MW01054390

WHAT INDUSTRY EXPERTS ARE SAYING

"I have always taught sales pros to develop ways to go the extra mile. It's critical to be not only memorable but memorable because of the level of service you provide to your clients. In this book, Lee has compiled excellent strategies for doing just that."

—TOM HOPKINS, Author of
How to Master the Art of Selling and *The Language of Sales*

"The perfect book for these new times. *Sells Different!* is a roadmap for sales success today and tomorrow with new strategies that will ensure victory in the only place that matters . . . your wallet. Lee has once again positioned you to get ahead and stay ahead of the emerging sales battlefield. Buy. Study. Implement."

—JEFFREY GITOMER,
Author of *The Little Red Book of Selling*

"Why blend into the crowd when you can stand out? Take it upon yourself to learn the concepts in this book so you stand out and close more deals. *Sell Different!* is a mandate for every seller who wants to win."

—ALICE HEIMAN,
Chief Sales Energizer, Alice Heiman, LLC

"Finally, the answers you've been looking for in one place. Lee puts it all right here and, best of all, delivers it in a way you can easily understand. The content is so good, *Sell Different!* won't be a book you read just once but a resource for you to access for months and years to come."

—MARK HUNTER,
"The Sales Hunter"

"As soon as I read *Sell Different!*, I knew that I was going to add it to our sales curriculum at Kansas State. Lee offers implementable ideas that drive performance."

—DAWN DEETER-SCHMELZ, PhD, J.J. Vanier
Distinguished Chair and Director, National Strategic
Selling Institute, Kansas State University

"To create, advance, and close more sales, you need to be different. Lee is the master at helping salespeople, and *Sell Different!* is packed with powerful, proven strategies and engaging stories to help you up your sales game and stand out from the competition."

—MIKE WEINBERG,
Author of *New Sales. Simplified.* and *Sales Management. Simplified.*

"In today's sales environment, the best way to cut through the noise and stand out is to sell differently. In *Sell Different!*, Lee lays out the specific tactics sales pros can use right away to not only get through to more buyers and win more deals but also do so at YOUR price."

—ART SOBCZAK,
Author of *Smart Calling*

"We have clearly entered a new phase in business growth and commercial relationships, and Lee's latest book, *Sell Different!*, has captured how to make that transition. One of the many messages that struck home with me was how sellers need to know, more than ever, how to harness the potential of virtual selling and remote conversations."

—BERNADETTE MCCLELLAND,
Commercial Conversations Academy™

"When you read *Sell Different!*, you will know how to differentiate the ways you sell. And differentiation—at least the way Lee teaches it—will leave your competitors in the dust."

—ROBERT W. BLY,
Author of *The Copywriter's Handbook*

"It doesn't matter what you're selling, to whom you're selling, or how long you've been selling . . . you need to read *Sell Different!*, absorb the concepts, and apply them to your selling repertoire. HOW you sell is as important—or more important—than WHAT you sell."

—NANCY NARDIN,
Founder, Smart Selling Tools, Inc.

"*Sell Different!* is a masterful book, providing a wealth of ideas for how to differentiate the right way and win more deals at the prices you want."

—MIKE SCHULTZ,
President, RAIN Group and Author of
Not Today: The 9 Habits of Extreme Productivity

"*Sell Different!* is truly refreshing since it is packed with immediately actionable tips and techniques that any sales professional can use to sell more. I highly recommend this book to anyone, no matter the industry. This is a universal guide to championship selling."

—**GERHARD GSCHWANDTNER**,
Founder and CEO, *Selling Power* magazine

"What is different about *Sell Different!* is what it isn't. It isn't another tip, hack, or technique to memorize. This book flips the script with actionable steps that put the focus on the buying experience we create as sellers and business owners, making it all about them, not about us."

—**CAROLE MAHONEY**,
Founder, Unbound Growth

"*Sell Different!* provides many innovative strategies and tactics to sidestep the most dangerous traps in today's B2B sales. From prospecting through account management, Lee walks you through the sales lifecycle, dispelling myths and revealing best practices all along the way."

—**JASON JORDAN**,
Bestselling Author of *Cracking the Sales Management Code*

"Your prospective clients are deciding whether to buy from you or your competitors. If you want them to choose you, the powerful strategies Lee presents in *Sell Different!* will make it clear you are different in a meaningful way so you get the deals at the prices you want."

—**ANTHONY IANNARINO**, Author of *Eat Their Lunch: Winning Customers Away from Your Competition*

"I found so much clarity in ways to *Sell Different!* and stand out among the strong competition we all have to face today. I counted dozens and dozens of practical ideas to try."

—**LORI RICHARDSON**,
CEO, Score More Sales, and President, Women Sales Pros

"Sales books come and go. Some stick, some don't. *Sell Different!* is here to stay. Packed with relevant techniques that sales professionals can use straight out of the book, right now!"

—**SIMON HARES**, International Sales Professional and Sales Coach, SerialTrainer7 Ltd.

"Lee continues to have his finger on the pulse of the ever-changing sales world and, with *Sell Different!*, he delivers another winner as he lays out how to differentiate yourself and stand out from the pack—regardless if you're new to sales or a sales veteran!"

—LARRY REEVES,
COO, American Association of Inside Sales Professionals

"To get the most from *Sell Different!*, you must first commit to be different. Take Lee's advice and examples, and put them into each and every part of your sales work."

—ANTHONY PARINELLO, Bestselling Author of
Selling to VITO (the Very Important Top Officer)

"*Sell Different!* reveals insights applicable to everyone from the first-time entrant into the sales profession to the seasoned sales leader looking to expand their sales base and win more deals. The foundational nature of this book will serve as the basis on which my sales program curriculum will be built to help our students master sales differentiation strategy."

—TODD WILLIAMS, Executive Director, Center for
Sales Leadership and Education, University of Minnesota

"As a long-term proponent of 'genuine sales,' it was refreshing to read the stories and examples Lee shares in *Sell Different!* to support an ethical way to help your buyers decide that your solution is the right one for them."

—NANCY BLEEKE,
Award-winning Author of *Conversations That Sell*
and Developer of the Genuine Sales suite of courses

"Lee brings a whole new perspective to modern-day sales. I love his holistic approach to the sales process, and his practical, common-sense style makes his concepts easy to understand and apply to everyday situations. I know firsthand that Lee's principles work in the real world—we worked with Lee to apply the strategies and techniques in *Sell Different!* and set all-time sales records in the process. If Lee's strategies can work in the motorcycle industry, they can work for any business."

—JIM WOODRUFF,
CEO, National Powersport Auctions

"Lee does it again with *Sell Different!* He creatively positions how to connect with your prospects by developing relationships based on simple, actionable concepts that make your audiences feel acknowledged, heard, and comfortable with the sales process. As a fifteen-year sales rep and now business owner in the transportation industry, I have been successful by applying these techniques with my team as our industry has been heavily commoditized. *Sell Different!* provides us with the tools to find valued clients at the prices we want. This is truly a must-read for anyone in the sales profession."

—NICOLE GLENN,
CEO, Candor Expedite, Inc.

"Salespeople can't just rely on their products' differentiators to gain buyer attention and stand out from the competition. They need to think different to add value, which means they need to sell different. Lee's new book gives you the tools to do just that. Apply these strategies to your selling, and you'll experience success at levels you never dreamed imaginable."

—BRANDON STEINER,
Former Founder, Steiner Sports, and Founder,
CollectibleXchange and AthleteDirect.com

"If you want to get your sales team off on the right foot, be sure they read *Sell Different!* Being different doesn't guarantee being better. But in this case, Lee coaches differentiation from the perspective of the client and what they value. Deploy the tactics Lee teaches here and watch your sales team achieve better results by being different where it counts: in your client's mind."

—TIM RETHLAKE,
Vice President of Trade Marketing and Sales Training,
Hearth & Home Technologies

"*Sell Different!* is loaded with strategies that work. I've seen our sales team penetrate our existing accounts by implementing Lee's strategies. There's no doubt the selling environment is changing fast, and using *Sell Different!* will give you that competitive advantage."

—DAVE KIRSCH,
President and CEO, Shippers Supply, Inc.

"The strategies Lee presents in *Sell Different!* have inspired and revolutionized our sales team. He is a significant reason for our company's growth to become one of the leading IT distributors in Australia. Lee's techniques, easy to understand and put into practice, have helped turn our sales team performance from good to great. Not only have they helped our company grow significantly, his teachings have given motivation to our sales team to really enjoy their roles."

—THEO KRISTORIS,
CEO, Leader Systems

"There are several hundred people in my company who are involved in direct sales. Lee's teaching in *Sell Different!* about our 'toughest competitor' offers great insight. I am confident this will help our direct salespeople to overcome their 'fear factor' related to competitors."

—JERRY L. MILLS,
CEO of B2B CFO® and Author of *The Exit Strategy Handbook*

"Nothing in *Sell Different!* is theoretical. How do I know that? Because we contracted with Lee, and he implemented these strategies and concepts in our company. The result? Record-setting sales month after month and explosive growth during a pandemic. If you are serious about moving forward in your sales efforts, don't just read the book. Embrace its teachings."

—DARYL HANCOCK,
Strategy and Execution Executive for more than twenty years

"*Sell Different!* will permanently change your sales results. I've seen many of Lee's techniques in action with a shared client. They've won close to 100 percent of their bids since implementing these strategies. They work!"

—BARBARA WEAVER SMITH, PhD,
Founder and CEO, The Whale Hunters

"*Sell Different!* presents subtle shifts in positioning, mindsets, and behaviors that can unlock significant untapped growth opportunities. This book is timely, as all sales leaders are looking to redesign and adapt sales management strategies for the changed markets—never a better time than now to focus on 'skill practice' to hone our skills and capabilities."

—MARK KNUREK,
Sales and Marketing Leader, Lubrizol Advanced Materials

"*Sell Different!* addresses the 'what to do' and 'why' when it comes to sales. Each chapter brings up key points that can be added to your sales team agenda and practiced for improvement to optimize sales. I truly wish that I had read this book twenty-five years ago, as it gives a step-by-step process to handle many challenges with solutions regarding selling."

—ROBERT FONTAINE,
Founder and President, Upstate Door, Inc.

"In minor league baseball, we focus on the guest experience to create loyal fans. In *Sell Different!*, Lee provides us with the recipe to differentiate the buying experience so we can convert fans into satisfied members who return with big smiles season after season."

—SUSAN SAVAGE,
Majority Owner, Sacramento River Cats

"*Sell Different!* is the definitive playbook for salespeople who want to take control of their earning power. It doesn't matter how competitive your industry is; in the end, success or failure depends on how you sell, not what you sell. Lee lays out the strategies that work in every sale. It's all about selling differently than the average salesperson. Don't worry, though—this process doesn't create more work. It simply reduces the time, rejection, and stress."

—KEVIN HILL,
Host of *Put That Coffee Down* podcast and Executive Publisher, FreightWaves

"Our industry has fallen into the trap of declining revenue per sale, as 'price selling' becomes a larger and larger theme. As we are breaking into new geographies and hunting new client relationships, each requires several of the proven strategies presented in *Sell Different!*"

—TRENT ANDERSON,
Vice President of Sales, LS Networks

"Building from the key insights he provides for sales professionals in *Sales Differentiation*, Lee has struck gold with *Sell Different!* Lee lays out clear and concise sales strategies and then ties them to key concepts that all sales teams need to be great at in order to consistently win. If you want to win more of the right deals on the right terms, this is a playbook to get you there."

—SHANNON BIBBEE,
Senior Vice President of Sales, Majestic Steel USA

"Lee brings actionable value to the sales world in *Sell Different!* People buy what they deem to be valuable, and instead of playing defense and rebuking objections, sellers need to focus on honing their craft to show and impact value to their buyers. Lee gives tips and tricks and insights that sellers can start to use immediately with success."

—WILL FRATTINI,
Sales Director, ZoomInfo

SELL
DIFFERENT!

ALL NEW SALES DIFFERENTIATION
STRATEGIES TO OUTSMART, OUTMANEUVER,
AND OUTSELL THE COMPETITION

LEE B. SALZ

HARPERCOLLINS
LEADERSHIP

AN IMPRINT OF HARPERCOLLINS

Published by HarperCollins Leadership, an imprint of HarperCollins Focus LLC.

Any internet addresses, phone numbers, or company or product information printed in this book are offered as a resource and are not intended in any way to be or to imply an endorsement by HarperCollins Leadership, nor does HarperCollins Leadership vouch for the existence, content, or services of these sites, phone numbers, companies, or products beyond the life of this book.

ISBN 978-1-4002-2251-3 (eBook)
ISBN 978-1-4002-2250-6 (HC)

Library of Congress Control Number: 2021939015

Printed in the United States of America
21 22 23 24 25 LSC 10 9 8 7 6 5 4 3 2 1

To my children, Jamie, Steven, and David

If there is one thing I hope you have learned from me, it's the importance of family. Your family gives you unconditional love, supports your ventures, and helps you grow as a person. They are your foundation, the people you can count on, and the ones who will be there for you no matter what. I love the way you support one another. Never stop!

To my wife, Sharon

I would not have accomplished what I have without you. Thank you for challenging me to be the best person I can be.

To my parents, Joseph and Myra Salz

Thank you for your support of everything I've ever tried to accomplish!

To my sister, Marlo Salz

Everyone should be as blessed as I am to have a sister like you. You rock!

To my in-laws, Paul and Gail Pershes

Thank you for supporting me in my ventures.

CONTENTS

ACKNOWLEDGMENTS

Many people contributed to the creation of *Sell Different!* and I'm forever grateful for their involvement in this book venture:

- Dawn Deeter-Schmelz, J.J. Vanier Distinguished Professor and Director, National Strategic Selling Institute, Kansas State University

- Todd Williams, Executive Director, Center for Sales Leadership and Education, University of Minnesota

- Mike Moroz, CEO, Walters Recycling and Refuse, Inc.

- Sharon Salz, my wife and rock-star editor

- Myra Salz, my mom and editor extraordinaire

- Louis Greenstein, superstar developmental and copy editor

My sincere thanks to all my clients and their salespeople who have embraced my Sales Differentiation philosophy to win more deals at the prices you want.

Thank you to Jack Daly for contributing an outstanding foreword for *Sell Different!*

I've known Lee Salz for more than fifteen years. My beliefs on how the best sales professionals achieve consistent results in any market are more aligned with his than with any other sales trainers that I'm aware of. That said, it wasn't until I read the draft of *Sell Different!* that I discovered we grew up just a few miles from each other in New Jersey, so maybe there was something in the water that resulted in our sharing such beliefs. A snapshot of my background will provide helpful context. Between the ages of twenty-six and forty-six, as an entrepreneur, I built six startups into national companies. All were fast-growing and my largest sales team numbered 2,600. Since then I have traveled the globe, helping companies and salespeople to outperform their competitors, following street-tested selling systems and processes. That's the key! What the reader will find in Lee's *Sell Different!* are the tools for salespeople to enjoy success in today's market. I'm honored to contribute this foreword to such a powerful sales book, which builds upon the foundation laid in his previous work, *Sales Differentiation.*

Sell Different! is packed with real-world action items, many of which can be put into place immediately upon reading. And I can authoritatively tell you that most salespeople are not employing them. That said, if you take the actions detailed here by Lee, you can't help but increase your sales results and your personal income. You will outmaneuver, outsmart, and outsell the competition. This book clearly exhibits Lee's commitment to the selling profession grounded in proven systems and processes. I frequently declare that "sports teams are run better than most businesses," as they all operate with a playbook and are well practiced on that playbook. Well, in *Sell Different!* Lee provides much of the guts from which you can build your sales playbook!

Some of my personal favorites (of which there are many), include:

- Proactive prospecting processes.
- Leveraging the power of referrals.
- Selling effectively to committees.
- Best implementation of a pilot program.
- Foolproof email strategies.
- Making the issue of "price" irrelevant.

As this important book goes to print, the world is challenged with a pandemic. Many of our businesses need to transition to selling virtually. Lee provides us the map to success here, and takes what many are seeing as drudgery and flipping it into a competitive advantage.

The best salespeople recognize that success has more to do with asking good questions than it does about crafting the best "pitch." Not only does Lee provide us with a menu of effective questions to consider, but better yet, he provides actual exercises we can perform to get better at this critical sales component.

Many of us are confronted with the big challenge of getting the interested prospect to indeed make the change from their current provider to a new relationship with us. For many, staying with the "known" is the much safer play. No worries. Lee has that covered as well, and his process here should be in every organization's sales playbook.

As I read *Sell Different!* I discovered another thing Lee and I have in common: we are rabid fans of the TV series *Law & Order*. For any of you who are fans as well, you know that the foundation of the shows are built around the discovery process. Both Lee and I are devoted viewers of the show because we both enjoy traveling the discovery process to see if we can solve the mystery. In many ways, this is parallel with what we need to do when we sell: it's all about the process of discovering the prospects' pains and pleasures, and helping them accordingly. In *Sell Different!* Lee Salz has handed us the process. All that is needed is for us to take action and "*Sell Different!*"

—*Jack Daly*
Sales Trainer, CEO Coach,
and Amazon Bestselling Author

INTRODUCTION:
MY INSPIRATION FOR
SALES DIFFERENTIATION
STRATEGY

There are plenty of books to help further your sales career. As you consider reading *Sell Different!* you may be asking yourself, "Why this one?"

The sole reason to read this book is to learn how to *win more deals at the prices you want.* Competition has never been more fierce than it is today. The differences in products and services from one competitor to another are smaller than ever before. This is true in all business settings: business to business, business to consumer, and business to government.

While competition may be tough, business owners and executives still expect their salespeople to acquire new accounts while protecting margins. But how do you win more deals at the prices you want when the differences among products are so slight?

The solution is to outsmart, outmaneuver, and outsell the competition. Every chapter in this book reveals strategies, techniques, and tactics to do just that. *Sell Different!* has nothing to do with the product, service, or technology you are selling, and everything to do with the ways you sell.

My commitment to you is that you will come away from reading *Sell Different!* with new ways to win more deals at the prices you want. If you read this book and it fails to meet that promise, email your purchase receipt to me at selldifferent@salesarchitects.com and I'll give you a full refund. How's that for a brand promise?

■ ■ ■

Differentiation Inspiration

I'm often asked how my passion for differentiation came about. Back in 1986, when I was a teenager growing up in Marlboro, New Jersey, a family friend named Dave offered me a summer job. Dave had come up with a creative business idea and asked me to work for him.

He had decided to start a pickup and delivery dry-cleaning service. Dave didn't own a dry-cleaning store, but he saw an opportunity to develop a business around laundry transportation. He contracted with a few local dry-cleaning stores to perform the cleaning and hired me as his pickup and delivery driver.

In those days, none of the dry cleaners in my town offered pickup and delivery services. As Dave described the opportunity, I could see dollar signs in his eyes. His excitement was almost tangible.

In addition to being hungry for a paycheck, I was intrigued by Dave's business idea. He identified a problem, which was time management, and turned it into a business opportunity. He felt that people in our town were too busy to be bothered with dropping off and picking up their dry cleaning. It was something that people needed to do but didn't necessarily want to spend their time doing.

He envisioned a premium service. Clients were expected to pay a transportation fee on top of their cleaning bill. At age seventeen, I was genuinely curious about the potential success of this business. "Will people pay more for this service?" I wondered.

I sure hoped they would since this was my summer job!

Dave's selling strategy was key. He didn't try to convince people that his dry cleaning was better than others. Instead, he positioned a solution to their problem. He talked with prospective customers about the convenience of having clean dress clothes in their closets without ever having to visit a dry-cleaning store. Most people could relate to needing a dress shirt or a pair of pants and not having clean clothes to wear. Dave positioned the ease of them leaving a laundry bag full of dirty clothes on their doorstep and having us take care of the transportation, returning with clean garments.

The question of whether or not people would sign up for this service was answered fairly quickly. Those who worked locally or had someone at home who could handle dry cleaning transportation did not see value in this offering. They didn't see going to the dry cleaner as a hardship. To them, this service was not worth the price tag.

However, many businesspeople from Marlboro commuted to New York City. At the time, businesspeople wore suits to work. With a daily commute in excess of two hours each way, they treasured this service. Some even wished they had come up with the idea. I was certainly thankful for the business's success as I minted money that summer.

Three Sales Takeaways

Dry-cleaning pickup and delivery turned out to be more than just a summer job. I learned a lot about people's buying behavior and took away three important sales messages that I help clients implement today.

1. **Price is not the primary decision factor when people are making buying decisions.** The primary decision factor is value. If people see value in what you are selling, they will buy at the prices you want. The burden of demonstrating that value sits on the shoulders of you, the salesperson.
2. **Know your audience.** What you sell might not be of interest to everyone. In this case, it clearly wasn't. Salespeople need to gain clarity on who will see value in what they offer. This helps avoid wasting time chasing deals that will either never be won or will only be won at prices you *don't* want.
3. **Identify your business's meaningful differentiators.** Without them, no one will see value in the offering. There are many ways to differentiate, and successful businesspeople are

insatiable in their search for those opportunities. While possessing differentiators is important, the critical part is being able to help someone on the other side of the desk become just as passionate as you are about those differentiators. Without that transfer of passion, buyer decisions come down to one factor: *price.*

Sales Differentiation

That summer job inspired my passion for Sales Differentiation, but the development of the overall strategy took a few decades to refine. I introduced it in my previous book, *Sales Differentiation.* That book is broken into two parts. The first half presents strategies to differentiate *what you sell.* Each chapter helps salespeople identify differentiators and develop communication strategies to position them with buyers in meaningful ways.

The second half of the book is about *how you sell* Sales Differentiation strategies. It delves into various phases of the new client acquisition process to uncover ways to provide meaningful value that the competition does not. The core purpose of both *what you sell* and *how you sell* Sales Differentiation strategies is to help you win more deals at the prices you want.

In *Sell Different!* I expand upon the *how you sell* side of the Sales Differentiation equation. You do not need to have read *Sales Differentiation* to understand *Sell Different!*

If you have an autographed copy of *Sales Differentiation,* you may have noticed I inscribed it with "Sell Different!" knowing that there would be a second book on the subject. It's also why all of my *Sales Differentiation* social media posts have the hashtag #selldifferent. While it may appear to be marketing, my intention was to challenge your thinking about the way you sell and inspire you to search for ways to differentiate beyond what your product offers. Search no more. I'm about to teach you how to win more deals at the prices you want.

Let's get started!

CHAPTER 1

DIFFERENTIATING THE BUYING EXPERIENCE AND CREATING "WOW!"

My son Steven played on his high school baseball team. While he was a darn good player, he also maintained a high grade point average. As talented a player as he was, no one could have predicted what would happen between his junior and senior years of high school.

That summer, Steven was selected to play on our city's American Legion baseball team. The team played in a tournament that attracted college baseball coaches from throughout the Midwest. During that one-week tournament, he hit four home runs and three doubles. What better time for him to be red hot than when college baseball coaches, who were scouting talented players, were in attendance.

Pretty soon, universities began to call Steven, inviting him to visit their campuses. Seven colleges were actively recruiting him. We knew he would face a tough decision a few months down the road. Each of the schools offered the major he wanted and was in his desired location. Their tuitions were all in the same ballpark. How would Steven decide which school to select?

■ ■ ■

1

Predicament or Opportunity

If you have ever been through a college athlete recruiting process, you know that it is pure sales. The coaches are attempting to sell athletes on their institutions, but they have a significant limitation when trying to stand out from other schools. They can't differentiate what they sell. They can't add a major, create a dormitory, or move the campus. All of those are fixed assets. Their only creative selling option is to leverage Buying Experience *Sell Different!* strategy, which differentiates not the product, but the purchasing process. When salespeople take that approach, they create an enormous opportunity to outsell the competition because the emphasis is on their buyers, not on themselves.

Few college baseball coaches would ever describe themselves as salespeople, but that is exactly who they are when they are recruiting student-athletes. That is by no means a negative description. It's a job requirement. Because coaches are held accountable for constructing a team of top talent, recruiting is a key factor of their success. They need to sell in-demand players on attending their institutions, but they face a lot of competition.

Many of us in sales are in the same predicament as these coaches. Since what we are selling is often very similar (or even identical) to our competitors, we have no opportunity to differentiate our products. But we are held accountable for success and are expected to win deals at the prices we want.

Realtors can't differentiate what they sell. There is a fixed inventory of houses on the market that they can offer to buyers, just as their competitors can. They can't differentiate the houses. How does someone pick one realtor over another when they all have the same products?

Another example is salespeople in the staffing industry. They can't differentiate what they sell either. They are selling "people" who can work for any staffing firm. These salespeople can try to argue that their people are *better* than their competitor's people, but who would believe that?

How does one select a staffing firm when all staffing firms sell the same product?

This is a tough selling predicament. Or is it really a predicament at all? In fact, it's an opportunity that many salespeople don't take advantage of, at least not at the levels they should. They are so heavily focused on trying to differentiate what they sell that they forget they also have an opportunity to stand out from the competition when they *Sell Different!* Just like salespeople, some college coaches were fantastic leveraging Buying Experience *Sell Different!* strategy while others failed miserably.

The Only One

Have you ever noticed that when you visit a college your blood pressure jumps thirty points as soon as you enter the campus? Finding a parking spot where you won't get ticketed or towed is like finding a needle in a haystack. The parking fiasco creates immediate irritation upon arrival at a time when your emotions are already running high.

One school we visited turned the parking hassle into a Buying Experience *Sell Different!* strategy opportunity. As we pulled into the lot at Hamline University, we were greeted by a sign on a parking stall with Steven's name on it. When we saw the sign, we just looked at one another, speechless! It certainly grabbed our attention and put smiles on our faces. What an incredible first impression!

We went inside for the university tour and were greeted by the head baseball coach, Jim Weyandt. He handed us an itinerary for the day; it had our son's name printed at the top of the page. Right from the first moments of the visit, this coach differentiated the buying experience. He created "Wow!"

What did it cost Hamline University to do those two things? A penny for the ink and paper? Because of those two small, thoughtful tactics, this college made us feel like Steven was the only athlete they were recruiting. Of course, that wasn't the case, but that's how we were made to feel.

Coach Weyandt described his strategy this way:

> "I'm sensitive to the anxiety both the players and their families feel during the recruiting process. I take steps to make both a great first and last impression to reduce their anxiety and make them feel special. The parking sign and agenda are ways we create a strong first impression. I also make a point to meet with each athlete and their family at the end of the visit to answer questions and address any concerns they may have. My first and last impression strategy is intended to make every athlete who visits our institution feel special and has been a key reason why we attract top talent to our program."

Salespeople and their companies have the same opportunity that Coach Weyandt described. We get caught up in our daily work and forget to make every Decision Influencer feel special. A Decision Influencer (DI) is someone who influences the decision-making process for what you sell. Throughout the book, I'll use the expressions "DI" and "buyer" interchangeably.

To leverage the Buying Experience *Sell Different!* strategy, salespeople need to make every DI feel special. No one likes to feel like a number. Clients want to feel special and appreciated. Salespeople achieve that through the buying experience they create.

Not enough executives and salespeople think about the buying experience as an opportunity to *Sell Different!* Yet, that strategy can be the key to win more deals at the prices you want. This is especially important when you can't differentiate what you sell. In the absence of differentiation, price is the prevailing decision factor. That's only good news if you are the low-price provider in your industry.

Most new client acquisition processes are designed to achieve one specific outcome, which is winning deals at the prices you want. Of course, that is the correct desired outcome. The flaw is in the process design. When creating the new client acquisition process, all too often the dominant vantage point is from the seller's side of the desk. Few consider the buyer's perspective. To take advantage of Buying Experience *Sell Different!* strategy, the new client acquisition process needs to take into account a decision maker's point of view as well. That perspective is revealed by asking yourself,

> **"In each phase of the buying process, what can I do different from my competitors that my DIs will find meaningful?"**

Every interaction you have with a buyer provides you with opportunities to use Buying Experience *Sell Different!* strategy. The best news I can share with you is that your competitors probably aren't considering that perspective, so take advantage of their shortcomings.

There are many ways to take advantage of Buying Experience *Sell Different!* strategy just as the head baseball coach at Concordia St. Paul University did.

Three Keys to *Sell Different!*

Concordia St. Paul University was another one of the schools recruiting Steven. They, too, were masterful with Buying Experience *Sell Different!* strategy, but approached it differently from Hamline University.

As part of the recruiting process, former athletic director and head baseball coach Mark "Lunch" McKenzie invited Steven to one of their practices to observe the program. While he was in the dugout, the players made him feel like a celebrity. One by one, they came up to him, introduced themselves, and struck up a conversation.

McKenzie described the school's recruiting approach this way:

> "As a Division II university, we are competing for top talent, not just with other universities at the same level, but also with Division I institutions. Those other schools may have more

resources at their disposal than we do, but no school will demonstrate being genuine, at a greater level, than our coaching staff.

"The foundation of our recruiting approach is based on the recognition that this isn't just a ballplayer we are recruiting; it is also someone's son. That mindset helps our coaching staff put together a recruiting experience that we would want for our own children.

"It is this foundation that leads to the core philosophy of our athlete recruiting process: make each player feel special, be genuine, and be responsive. Blended together, those differentiate us and form our competitive advantage when recruiting top talent."

What Coach McKenzie shared isn't just a nice college athlete recruiting story. There's an important message that every salesperson should embrace.

Over the years, I have had the opportunity to interview buyers about their frustrations with salespeople. Their three biggest complaints are that salespeople don't make them feel special, they aren't genuine, and they aren't responsive. The three points that Coach McKenzie cites as his keys to winning can be yours as well.

Make your DIs and clients feel special. Be genuine. Be responsive.

None of those three points require you to differentiate what you sell, nor do they cost you or your company a penny. You also don't need your company or even your sales manager to do anything for you to put this into practice today. You, as an individual revenue contributor, can make changes in your sales game to take advantage of Buying Experience *Sell Different!* strategy now. Make your DIs and clients feel special. Be genuine. Be responsive. Implementing these approaches can help you hit your quota out of the ballpark.

You can also tell, based on Coach McKenzie's statement, that he looks at the process from the buyer's perspective, not just his own. By inviting recruits to watch a practice, he is immersing them in the university's culture and making them feel like they are already involved in the program. He knows that experience helps "buyers" make informed decisions.

The automotive industry is among several that are masterful at leveraging Buying Experience *Sell Different!* strategy. New car salespeople excel at it. One of the very first steps of their process is to have you take a test drive. They want you to feel as if you own the car. As you come back to the showroom after the drive, they are looking for that smile, which tells them you loved the driving experience. By placing you in the driver's seat rather than taking you through a sales process, the salesperson creates a buying experience.

The home furniture industry is another example. Top furniture salespeople leverage Buying Experience *Sell Different!* strategy. They don't just show a buyer a couch. They ask the buyer to sit on the couch and they leave the family to have a conversation among themselves as if they were in their own living room. Think about the layout of most furniture showrooms. Instead of rows and rows of couches, they are strategically positioned throughout the store in living room settings. This creates a buying experience for a family who can feel what it would be like to have the couch, and perhaps the rest of the living room furniture, in their home.

The software industry does this too. Top software product salespeople don't just demonstrate the product to DIs. They have the DIs use the product, with their guidance, as part of the buying experience. This allows them to experience the tools and know what it would be like to own the product.

Authenticity

Augsburg University was another one of the schools recruiting Steven. On the day we visited, it was raining. Their head baseball coach, Keith

Bateman, asked Steven to text him upon our arrival. Shortly afterward, a group of assistant coaches carrying umbrellas greeted us in the parking lot and escorted us into the facility.

Coach Bateman didn't start the day with a tour, but with a conversation over coffee to discuss Steven's ambitions and desires in academics as well as baseball. Rather than have an admissions counselor show us the campus, Coach Bateman took us on the tour. He spent almost four hours with us that day and made Steven feel like he was already part of the program.

Following the visit, Steven and the coach exchanged texts and phone calls seemingly on a weekly basis. Coach Bateman invited Steven to visit the campus again, but this time it was to have dinner with several of the players and attend a women's volleyball game.

When he was accepted to Augsburg University, he didn't find out from a form letter in the mail. Coach Bateman called and said, "Welcome to Augsburg University," and Steven excitedly accepted!

I had the opportunity to interview Coach Bateman about his recruiting approach. I recounted our "buying experience" as we evaluated the university. As we talked, it became apparent that none of what we experienced during the process was accidental. Every bit of it was intentional. Given the level of competition he faces for top players at a Division III university, he recognizes a need for an approach that stands out. He described his strategy this way:

> "When I think about our overall recruiting approach, I can sum it up in one word: *authentic*. It's a word that is easy to say but requires your heart to truly embrace it.
>
> I don't look at my time with a player as a four-year engagement. To me and my coaching staff, this is a forty-plus-year relationship with the player and family.
>
> Authentic means I have to build a relationship and establish trust with each player. And I recognize how I do those two things needs to be different for each player. I don't just do those things during the recruiting process to get a player to agree to

come to Augsburg University. Authentic is not a tactic; it's who I am and who I expect my coaches to be as well.

I take pride in building relationships with every player on the team. I call them on their birthdays. They hear from me on holidays. They know if they are having difficulty with a class, a teammate, or anything in their life that I am here to help. Without me asking them to do it, players share those stories with recruits and it truly matters to the prospective athletes.

When we are recruiting, our key strategy is communication. Recruits hear from us every seven to ten days during the process. We aren't doing this to force a decision, but rather to get to know the players and for them to get to know us. Communication doesn't end as the recruiting process concludes, but rather is part of our authenticity. I believe communication is the cornerstone of relationship development.

Last year, I took our baseball team to Cuba for a baseball experience. Due to US/Cuba relations, parents were not permitted to go on the trip. The level of trust a parent had to have in me to allow their son to take this trip is not something I take lightly. Without our authenticity mindset, we would not have been able to take the team to Cuba.

I take great pride in the fact that I, and my coaches, have developed strong relationships with our players through authenticity. It is authenticity that leads prospective players to select our institution."

Webster's defines "authenticity" as *the quality of being genuine.* Coach Bateman's Buying Experience *Sell Different!* strategy is founded in relationship development based on his authenticity. He faces immense competition for players at the Division III level and he brilliantly uses the buying experience to attract players to his team.

Few new client acquisition processes emphasize relationship development, but it is a critical part of the buying experience. Actually, relationship development is a result of a properly designed buying experience. Most new client acquisition processes are comprised of questions for salespeople to ask and information they need to share with buyers. Few salespeople ask themselves:

> **"What can I do during the new client acquisition process to build a strong relationship with my buyers?"**

What Coach Bateman teaches us with his recruiting approach is the importance of authenticity when selling. How can salespeople be authentic with buyers? Just as Coach said, it has to come from the heart. Salespeople who put their wallet before the needs of their clients fail in sales.

Top salespeople recognize that putting their DIs' needs before their own is a key to their success. This becomes apparent during the buying experience.

Top salespeople recognize that putting their DIs' needs before their own is a key to their success.

I'm sure you've heard countless times that people buy from those they like, trust, and find sincere. As Coach Bateman put it, "Those words are easy to say, but require your heart to truly embrace it."

Coach Bateman also mentioned a key to his success is communication. He doesn't wait for recruits to call him. He contacts them and shows genuine interest in each prospective player. Salespeople struggle with this concept. Many are afraid to send an email or make a phone call to buyers because they feel they will come across as "salesy." If you are authentic in your approach, that will never happen to you. You won't dial a number or put your hands on a keyboard unless you have something that will be perceived by the buyer as meaningful and helpful for the buying experience.

Just a Number

Interestingly, none of these schools were on Steven's radar screen when the college recruiting process began. The school that was at the top of his list at the beginning of the process was at the bottom of the list when the process concluded. He loved that school's campus, but their baseball coach didn't do any of the things that coaches Weyandt, McKenzie, or Bateman did. That coach relied on the school's brand to attract players. He was supposedly interested in having Steven play for his team, but his actions didn't relay that message. While the other schools' coaches made Steven feel special, this coach made him feel like nothing but a number.

Just like that coach, salespeople sometimes get lazy with the buying experience. They rely on a strong brand or a great product to lead them to the win. That approach may work some of the time, not because of the salespeople, but despite them.

Your Success "at Steak!"

There's a steakhouse called Pittsburgh Blue in our Minnesota neighborhood. Sharon and I enjoy going there for date nights. While the food is very good, that isn't the sole reason we continue to dine there. At the crossroads where Pittsburgh Blue is located, there are six options for a juicy steak. How's that for competition?

Each one of those restaurants can grill a delicious steak, yet we continue to patronize Pittsburgh Blue time and time again. If you think it is because of price, you would be incorrect. Of the six options at that intersection, they are the most expensive.

The reason we keep going there is because of Sara, one of their servers. Whenever we make a reservation there, we ask to sit in Sara's section. She remembers both Sharon's and my favorite drink and brings them out shortly after we sit at her table. She remembers our names and even what we usually order for dinner. She's warm, friendly, and attentive. Most important, she understands why we are there. We want a relaxing, no-hassle meal and she creates that dining experience for us.

On some occasions, the steaks were not served as we ordered them, but each time she quickly remedied the situation. She even surprised us with complimentary desserts when that occurred. No business is perfect. Mistakes give you the opportunity to shine. Don't panic. It's not the end of the world. In most cases, it won't cost you a client, but it will give you an opportunity to show you care and make the situation right. It's all part of the Buying Experience *Sell Different!* strategy that you commit to delivering for your clientele.

My challenge to you is to create a buying experience that leads DIs to want to buy from you at the prices you want rather than from the competition. Here are ten opportunities to differentiate the buying experience. Many of these are explored in the subsequent chapters of this book.

1. Ways you handle prospecting outreach.
2. Information you send prior to discovery meetings, so they receive value.
3. Your approach to facilitating discovery meetings through questioning and information sharing.
4. Materials you provide after discovery meetings to help them make informed buying decisions.
5. Your handling of group presentations and demonstrations so they are informative, engaging, and interactive.
6. Ways you verbally share solutions with DIs.
7. How you design proposals to communicate solutions.
8. Your methods of handling pilot/trial programs.
9. How you structure contracts.
10. Your client onboarding program to transition them into your organization.

Put this book down for a moment. Take out paper and a pen. Write down three of these opportunities you feel can meaningfully differentiate the buying experience for your DIs. Select methods your competitors are not using so you can outsmart, outmaneuver, and outsell them.

BUYING EXPERIENCE *SELL DIFFERENT!* CONCEPT

Be genuine and make every Decision Influencer feel special, as if they are your only one throughout the buying experience.

CHAPTER 2

YOUR TOUGHEST COMPETITOR IS NOT WHO YOU THINK IT IS

One of my favorite questions to ask salespeople is, "*Who is your toughest competitor?*" I've posed this question to salespeople all around the world. Yet, I've never had any salesperson answer correctly.

Most salespeople quickly rattle off three names of players in their space who they see as competitors. "I'm sure those are tough competitors," I tell them. "But there is one even tougher."

Some salespeople think I'm asking a trick question. They'll recall a lesson they learned from a sales trainer years ago and venture a guess: "You mean the status quo, aka the choice to do nothing?" That is certainly a tough competitor, but there is one even tougher.

A few salespeople consider themselves as their biggest competitor. "If I don't have a strong mental game, I am my own worst enemy," they say. True! If you don't have the right sales mindset, you can be a limiting factor in your success. But you are not your own toughest competitor.

There is one even tougher, more formidable than any other. As I said, no one has ever figured out who that competitor is. The answer will shock you. It isn't going to make you feel better about your sales situation. Actually, it will make you uncomfortable, which believe it or not is a good thing. If you know who your toughest competitor is, you can take the actions necessary to defeat it.

So, who is your toughest competitor?

It's every salesperson calling the same Decision Influencer you are.

When we think about competition, we tend to be egocentric; we only consider it from our side of the desk. Let's flip it around to the Decision Influencer's side of the desk and see it from their perspective. The person you are calling is receiving prospecting calls and emails from salespeople representing the DI's entire purview of responsibilities. Each salesperson is selling the identical thing: "a meeting." They want phone or face time with the same person you seek to engage.

No executive is sitting at her desk, staring at her phone, and hoping it will ring with a salesperson on the other end.

Here's the bad news. You aren't competing against a handful of players in your industry, but against hundreds of salespeople who are calling on this DI.

Suppose you call on a CIO to sell application development services. Set aside for a moment the fact that there are a number of players in your industry. Now, think about a CIO's overall responsibilities. He is inundated with calls and emails from others in your space as well as from the telecom industry, hardware providers, software providers, and on and on. Among the hundreds of salespeople reaching out to him, how many will actually land a meeting? A few, maybe.

Here is a fact you might not know.

In the history of business, there has never been an executive hired for the sole purpose of meeting with salespeople every hour on the hour.

It's never happened! No executive is sitting at her desk, staring at her phone, and hoping it will ring with a salesperson on the other end. Let's face it: we are an interruption in her day. DIs have many responsibilities and they are only going to meet with a select few salespeople.

Here is an important sales dynamic of which to be mindful. If there isn't a meeting, there isn't a proposal. If there isn't a proposal, there is no sale. If there is no sale, there's no commission check. It's a very logical, yet scary, dynamic. If you are to be the one to secure the meeting, you need to leverage Prospecting *Sell Different!* strategy.

Prospecting Is Dead. Or Is It?

Some salespeople argue that prospecting is dead; that it's a waste of time. Perhaps you are in that camp. "Executives aren't going to buy from someone who contacted them through prospecting," you think. "The only thing that works is networking and referrals." While I agree that networking and referrals are important components of an effective overall business development strategy, they are not the only components you need. Prospecting cannot be ignored. It must be done religiously, a point that is further addressed in chapter 14.

The RAIN Group, a well-respected global sales training firm, conducted an intriguing survey among executives. Respondents were asked if they had ever accepted a meeting with a salesperson who reached out to them through prospecting. I love asking audiences to guess the percentage that accepted the meeting. One shouts out "6 percent!" Another guesses 15 percent. Others argue that's too low and insist it's 38 percent.

Based on the survey, all of those answers are wrong. The correct answer is 82 percent! Eighty-two percent of executives say they agreed to a meeting with a salesperson who contacted them through prospecting. Prospecting is alive and well. All salespeople need to include it in their business development repertoire.

■ ■ ■

Prospecting Controversy

Prospecting is performed a number of ways. One of the most common is picking up the phone and calling DIs. Based on my experiences, more than 90 percent of the time, salespeople aren't going to reach the DI, but rather their voicemail.

Voicemail is a controversial topic among salespeople. About half of them fervently argue never to leave a voicemail message when prospecting. The other half firmly believe in the practice. I get a kick out of watching this debate play out at sales conferences. Showing my age here, this debate reminds me of the famous Miller Lite commercials from the 1980s with two sides fanatical about their perspectives. "Tastes great!" "Less filling!" Want to have some fun at your next sales meeting? Ask the sales team what their thoughts are on leaving voicemail messages during prospecting. It's rather entertaining as both sides are passionate in their beliefs.

Those salespeople who believe in leaving voicemail messages when prospecting often have me scratching my head in confusion. They say they firmly believe in leaving voicemail messages, and yet, few have a documented strategy for doing so. Without a planned voicemail strategy, the messages are usually garbled with more "ums" than substance, which does not help the selling effort.

There's another point to consider when it comes to prospecting by voicemail. Let's say that you are so engulfed in this book, you just missed a phone call.

You check your voicemail messages and find one that says, "I have ten thousand dollars for you. Call me back!" If you are like most of my audiences, you aren't returning that call.

What if the message said, "I can cut your cell phone bills in half. Call me!" Are you returning that call? I'm guessing probably not.

How about if the message was, "I can reduce your interest rates by 5 percent. Let's talk!" You probably aren't calling this salesperson back either.

Here is the big question: What could a salesperson say in a voicemail message that would lead you to return the call?

In this scenario, one salesperson offered you a significant amount of money and that didn't do it. Two offered to reduce your costs and you didn't call them back either. So, what would it take for you to call a salesperson back?

Here is an unfortunate sales fact: there is only one instance when it is highly likely to receive a return call from a prospecting voicemail. It's when serendipity takes place. You happen to leave a message about a topic that is presently front of mind for the DI. For example, if you sell roofing and I just discovered I have a leak in my roof, I'll want to talk with you. Beyond that, the likelihood of a return call is slim.

> What could a salesperson say in a voicemail message that would lead you to return the call?

By now you probably think I'm against leaving voicemail messages when prospecting. If you believe that, you are incorrect. I'm a huge proponent of leaving voicemail messages when prospecting, but I believe we need to change our perspective on voicemail and use a Prospecting *Sell Different!* strategy.

Let's accept the fact that they aren't going to call back. Take it off the table. It isn't going to happen. You even say as much in your message. "I'm not expecting you to call me back." How many salespeople are saying that in their voicemail messages? Very few! It's different. It's compelling. While you aren't expecting a return call, of course, you still share your contact information in the message.

When leaving a voicemail message, it needs to accomplish two key objectives:

- Create intrigue.
- Provide context for your outreach.

Whet the DI's whistle with your message, so he has perspective for your call.

The RAIN Group survey also revealed the secret ingredient to acquiring a meeting through prospecting: personalization. DIs can smell a generic, unauthentic sales outreach a mile away. This is true in any form of prospecting, not just voicemail messages. In *Sales Differentiation,* I presented the concept of a Sales Crime Theory that differentiates you when prospecting and creates a qualitative approach for it. Before reaching out to a DI, the Sales Crime Theory challenges you to ask yourself this question: "Why should he want to have a conversation with me right now?" The answer to that question helps you shape a creative strategy for your prospecting outreach.

The Prospecting Rhythm

The key to prospecting success is both qualitative and quantitative. The qualitative side is the personalization I referenced before. What is equally important is the quantitative side. I won't bore you with statistics suggesting that salespeople are not making enough attempts to reach buyers. You've seen that a hundred times and I'm sure you get the point. But those studies just say you need to make more attempts; they don't tell you how to do it. I'm going to share a quantitative prospecting strategy with you that answers the question of how to reach DIs.

The first step is to shift your mindset about the way you think of prospecting. It is not an event, but a campaign. A successful campaign includes a number of creative techniques over a period of time to reach the desired DI.

I'm going to teach you a four-week outbound prospecting campaign with the intent of reaching and engaging the DI. The presumption, before you initiate the campaign, is that you have a reason for your outreach (Sales Crime Theory). If the sole purpose of your prospecting is to make a sale, don't waste your time or theirs. It won't work. You'll instantly turn them off.

While the prospecting campaign is four weeks in duration, there are only sixteen steps. Studies show prospecting on Mondays has a low likelihood to be effective. So, for starters, skip Mondays for your outreach.

The campaign uses multiple techniques including phone calls. Want to increase your batting average reaching DIs live rather than their voicemail boxes? Don't call them during business hours. Executives bounce from meeting to meeting between the hours of 9:00 a.m. and 5:00 p.m. It is highly unlikely that you will reach them during that time. Call before and after business hours to increase your chances of reaching them instead of their voicemail.

Also, before initiating this campaign, develop the core of the voicemail message you will use. Here are some keys to success in developing your voicemail message strategy.

- Leave room in the message core for message personalization.
- The message should be thirty seconds or less in duration. That means you need to avoid filler that provides no value. For example, let's say I leave a message that says, "Hi, Phil. This is Lee Salz from Sales Architects. I hope you are having a great day." The last sentence wasted three seconds. It's unnecessary. I assure you this stranger doesn't believe I care whether they are having a great day, so I'm not going to waste valuable seconds saying it.
- Before you leave the message, practice it. Then, practice it some more. Mastery of your message creates the positive, professional image you desire.
- Make sure you have phone energy when you deliver it, rather than coming across flat. You want to spark an interest with the DI so that he'll want to have a conversation with you. That means it's not just about the words you say, but how you say them. In chapter 5, I delve further into the importance of phone persona.

There is also an email component to this prospecting strategy. Develop a core email template for use in the campaign. Here are some keys to success in developing your email message:

- Be mindful of the subject line of the email. Without an engaging subject line, the DI will never open and read your email.
- Leave room in the message core for message personalization.
- Your message should be no more than two paragraphs. That means you need to avoid unnecessary words that provide no value.
- Keep the message focused on them, not on you, your company, or your products. If you talk about yourself, the message sounds like the hundreds of others they receive. Focusing on them means you *Sell Different!* and stand out from the masses.

Now that you have polished your voicemail, email, and live-contact prospecting messages, you are ready for my 16-Day Prospecting Campaign that provides strategy for the quantitative side of your prospecting game.

16-Day Prospecting Campaign

DAY 1: Send a personalized email to create intrigue. The message should give context to the outreach and the reason you are contacting her now (Sales Crime Theory). Be sure to make the message about her, not you.

DAY 2: Call and leave a voicemail message referencing the email you sent if you are unable to reach her live.

DAY 3: Call at a different time of day from the prior attempt, but don't leave a message.

DAY 4: Do not contact her today.

DAY 5: Call and leave a voicemail message referencing the email you sent if you don't reach her live.

DAY 6: Forward your original email message and add content to create more intrigue. Again, keep the message content focused on her, not you. Or, send a video email if you have access to that technology.

DAY 7: Call at a different time of day and leave a voicemail message if you don't reach her live. In your message, let her know when you will call again.

Here is a piece of gold! Send her a calendar invite for that date and time. In most email systems, when you send an invite, it appears in the recipient's calendar whether the invite is accepted or not.

As brilliant as that calendar invite prospecting technique is, I can't take credit for it. Lisa Chase, the best prospector I have ever had the privilege of knowing, has been using that technique, and it works! Over the years, I've seen her use this approach in a few different companies and industries. This technique is one of the gold nuggets she attributes to her prospecting success.

DAY 8: Call at the time you scheduled and leave a voicemail message if you don't reach her live.

DAY 9: Do not contact her today.

DAY 10: Send her a LinkedIn invite and include the same email content as the message you sent on day six.

DAY 11: Call at a different time of day and leave a voicemail message if you don't reach her live that tells her when you will call again. Send her a calendar invite for that time.

DAY 12: Call at the time you scheduled and leave a voicemail message if you don't reach her live.

DAY 13: Do not contact her today.

DAY 14: Call at a different time, but don't leave a message.

DAY 15: Call at a different time of day and leave a voicemail message if you don't reach her live that tells her when you will call again. Send her a calendar invite for that time.

DAY 16: Call at the time you scheduled and leave a voicemail message if you don't reach her live.

Some of you may have read this campaign and thought it was aggressive; maybe too aggressive. But consider the converse. Some salespeople only try to reach this DI a few times. You must have something really important to discuss if you are trying to reach her through so many creative methods. Combined with the Sales Crime Theory strategy, this prospecting campaign is extremely effective in helping salespeople reach and initiate conversations with DIs. Try it!

At the conclusion of the program, if you still haven't connected with her, cease calling for ninety days. Put her name in the "dead file" for now. You didn't reach her, but you can certainly feel comfortable knowing that you made a strong attempt. Your outreach might not have worked for this one person, but your overall prospecting success should be through the roof if you follow this prospecting campaign for every DI you want to reach!

By implementing these creative outreach techniques, your chances of reaching the person you want to connect with have skyrocketed. While the competition made a few lame attempts, you leveraged Prospecting *Sell Different!* strategy. You win!

PROSPECTING *SELL DIFFERENT!* CONCEPT

Successful prospecting strategy requires a thoughtful approach to both the qualitative and quantitative components.

CHAPTER 3

FINDING MORE OF YOUR BEST CLIENTS

D avid had a great sales year. He blew out his numbers. As a "thank-you" for his performance, his company increased his new business quota by 30 percent for this year. Now he'll have to win more deals than ever before. Where is he to find enough new clients to hit his numbers in the coming year?

In sales, we are all accustomed to this increase in expectation. "Whatever you did last year, we want more this year." That's the mantra heard in most companies. Challenging as it is for salespeople to accept that increase, it's a business necessity. Companies are either growing or dying. There isn't a status quo option. This challenge raises a question for executives, sales leaders, and salespeople: Where are we going to find this new business to grow at the desired level?

Gaining Clarity on the Clients You Want

Sales life would be pure bliss if salespeople could take their best clients, place them in a copier, and replicate them. Wouldn't that be awesome? Just press the copy button and, magically, a new best client is added to the company portfolio. Unfortunately, client replication isn't an option for sales.

Finding more of their best clients is a front-of-mind issue for sales leaders and salespeople. Sales leaders host brainstorming meetings in boardrooms. Salespeople search high and low. They go to random trade shows and conferences looking for more of their best clients. They seek them online, too.

Yet, business development doesn't need to be as hard as we make it.

In this chapter, I'm going to share a Business Development *Sell Different!* strategy with you that you probably have never heard of before. The sole purpose of this strategy is to help you find more of your best clients.

You may have noticed the repeated expression "more of your best clients" in this chapter. The reason is for emphasis. In most cases, your largest clients are not your best clients. Large clients serve an important purpose, perhaps as a foundation for your business. However, you might not want more of them. Some large clients require heavy customization that you don't want to provide in mass quantities. Others may be low-margin accounts or have other undesirable qualities.

The new accounts you want to pursue should align with your company's Target Client Profile. In chapter 6 of *Sales Differentiation*, I shared the nine components of this profile.

- **Size.** This can be revenue, employees, units—any quantification that provides focus on the right scope of opportunities to pursue.
- **Location.** This addresses the geography on which to focus selling efforts.
- **Business type.** This refers to industry types (NAICS codes) and business structure (public or private) for the type of business you desire.
- **Incumbent.** This is the list of providers that have inferior/ incomplete products and services compared to what you offer.

- **Circumstances/goals.** This segment of the profile is achieved by completing these expressions. Our target client has issues with _____, a desire to _____, and/or _____ goals.
- **Decision drivers.** These are the factors that lead to exploration of adding to the current solution or replacing the current provider.
- **Corporate attributes.** This addresses corporate DNA, including financial health and corporate culture.
- **Buying process.** This identifies the alignment between how they buy and your opportunity to demonstrate meaningful value.
- **Deal breakers.** This is the converse of what you want in a target client; it includes aspects such as slow payer, public relations issues, not in geography where you operate, wants kickbacks, or other indicators that you do not want this business.

> **To download my Target Client Profile worksheet, visit www.TargetClientProfile.com**

Use these nine criteria to gain clarity on the right opportunities to pursue all day long. If you haven't developed this profile yet, you need to do so now! You won't be able to incorporate the strategy into your selling repertoire without it. Furthermore, salespeople may be wasting time, dollars, and resources pursuing deals that will never materialize.

I refer to the profile as "Target Client" rather than "Ideal Client" for one very important reason. "Ideal Client Profile" suggests a once-in-a-lifetime opportunity. If all the stars aligned, this is the perfect opportunity for the company. "Target Client Profile," however, conveys a different message to salespeople. It says this is the type of account we want you to pursue all day long. We don't expect this type of win on occasion. We expect this to be the primary account our salespeople invest their time pursuing. The Target Client Profile serves as the core selling focus for the sales team.

The Strategy

The first step of this Business Development *Sell Different!* strategy is to create a list of ten clients. These are clients whom you would replicate in a copier in a heartbeat if only you could. As mentioned before, they may not be your largest, but they are, by your own definition, your best clients.

The next step of the strategy is to identify who in your organization has the closest relationship with the highest-level Decision Influencer in the account. In a typical business-to-business (B2B) sales environment, this is likely the person who awarded you the contract. In business to consumer (B2C) sales, more often than not it's the person with whom you interacted the most during the new client acquisition process.

The third step is for the salesperson on your team who has the closest relationship with the DI to be tasked with having a live conversation with that individual. Notice I said, "live conversation." Emails and texts are not effective for this strategy. A live conversation with the DI should be held either on the phone or in person.

The conversation flows like this:

> **"Jamie, you have been a client of ours for a number of years, so you are familiar with what we offer and the quality of what we offer. May I ask you a question?**
> **If you were me . . .**
> **what associations would you be active in,**
> **what conferences would you attend,**
> **what events would you go to,**
> **what would you be reading,**
> **to meet more people like you?"**

I call this the "If You Were Me" Business Development *Sell Different!* strategy. Business development is like an open book test in school. We don't need to guess where to find more of our best clients. What we need to do is leverage our most precious resource, our clients, to acquire the answers. Ask and you shall receive!

During these conversations, you aren't asking for referrals, nor are you asking DIs to serve as references. You aren't upselling or cross selling your products and services either. The sole purpose of this conversation is to ask your trusted DI to place your hat on his head and provide you with insights and recommendations.

Note that you aren't asking what conferences they attend or what they read. That information is irrelevant. They might not have the budget to attend conferences or join associations. They might not enjoy reading. All you are requesting is their suggestions, nothing more, nothing less.

> The sole purpose of this conversation is to ask your trusted DI to place your hat on his head and provide you with insights and recommendations.

The phrase "meet more people like you" within the strategy is included because it strokes the DI's ego. It shows he is important. And, it conveys to the DI with whom you are looking to develop relationships. This is why the Target Client Profile is so important to have in place prior to enacting this strategy. If you don't have clarity about "your best client," it's impossible to find more of them.

Imagine asking the "If You Were Me" question of a CIO. That person likely knows which associations, conferences, and events are worthwhile and which are duds. This individual can point you in the right direction of what you should be reading as well.

If you are selling security systems to homeowners (a B2C sale), the "If You Were Me" strategy is a great way to gain insight about your clients. There may be neighborhood meetings or community events that they would recommend you attend. There may be newsletters you should be reading. If you don't pose that question, you'll have to guess where to find these people. Why guess when you can ask and be pointed in the right direction?

You will be astonished by the level of graciousness you will experience from your clients. Fundamentally, people love to help. It's in our nature, but we don't always volunteer to help. Sometimes we have to be asked.

You'll also be amazed by the sheer volume of insight you receive. Better have a pen and paper ready to take notes because your clients have a tremendous amount of information to share.

A key for this strategy to work properly is to provide cues within the question. That is why I specifically mentioned associations, conferences, events, and reading. These hints give context to the question and they help the DI quickly filter out information that's irrelevant to you.

> A key for this strategy to work properly is to provide cues within the question.

This strategy will provide you with new ideas and techniques to find more of your best clients whom you might not have considered. What's more, DIs can validate ideas you are exploring or have already implemented, helping you avoid making costly mistakes.

Results

This strategy has a 1.000 batting average. I am not exaggerating. I've never had a client incorporate this strategy into their business development approach and come away empty-handed. I'll share two of my favorite stories with you.

For one of my coaching clients, I tasked their team with initiating ten "If You Were Me" conversations over a two-week period. Just prior to our update call two weeks later, the sales manager sent me an apologetic email. "Due to other priorities, we were only able to complete four of these conversations." Within the email, he attached their findings. The document was four pages long, single-spaced. All of those findings were from just four conversations with clients! With that success, no apology was needed.

During our update call, the sales manager said he was holding off on conducting more of these conversations for the moment. They received so much wonderful information from the first four conversations that they wanted to incorporate it into their business development strategy before soliciting more information from clients.

I tasked another coaching client with this assignment as well. He completed seven "If You Were Me" conversations over two weeks. Based on those conversations, he had a forty-five-minute update for me, sharing everything he learned during those interactions.

He found out about a technology council that was right in his backyard that he didn't know existed. His client then offered, "I can bring you to one of our council meetings if you like." Absolutely! He took advantage of that opportunity and wound up presenting to a dozen CIOs that he had been dying to meet. Until that time, he had been unable to reach them through traditional prospecting means.

He conducted one of those seven "If You Were Me" conversations in person while his CEO was with him. The CEO didn't know about this strategy. Toward the end of the meeting, my coaching client posed the "If You Were Me" question to the DI. His CEO was floored! That night, the CEO sent me this brief email:

> **"Lee, it feels like this is the question I've been missing for the last fifteen years of my life. THANK YOU! Watched it in action today. Nearly cried. Spectacular."**

This strategy works! Best of all, what does it cost your company to put it into practice? ZERO! I'm not asking you to spend a nickel. You'll invest a little time and receive a wealth of information that can send your business soaring into the stratosphere.

Recommendation Processing

Once the team has been assigned to have the "If You Were Me" conversations, give them two weeks to complete them. Then follow these steps to process the recommendations received:

1. Host a meeting for the team members to share their findings. Include the management team in the meeting as well. They should hear the business development recommendations your clients have provided.

2. During the meeting, develop a master list of the recommendations. Highlight those that were shared by multiple clients, as duplication should garner further attention.

3. Develop action plans with accountabilities and timelines for those recommendations.

4. Regroup with the team every thirty days to update on progress.

The "If You Were Me" strategy is not a onetime initiative. Incorporate it into your account management and business review programs. Again, only pose this question to clients you want to replicate. Also, with clarity on your Target Client Profile, you can use this strategy with industry partners as they have keen insight into the information you seek.

You certainly have the option to ignore this strategy and continue prospecting the same way children play Pin the Tail on the Donkey: blindfolded. But why would you? There's no reward for working hard in sales, only for being effective.

BUSINESS DEVELOPMENT *SELL DIFFERENT!* CONCEPT

The "If You Were Me" strategy helps you find more of your best clients by leveraging Decision Influencer relationships that you already have.

CHAPTER 4

MAKING YOUR SALES LIFE EASIER
AND MORE LUCRATIVE

D uring the dot-com boom, I managed a sales team in the technology training industry for a company based just outside of Washington DC. The team was divided into three groups: corporate, government, and career changers. Given the rapid growth of technology, there was a tremendous skills gap in the marketplace, which created opportunities for those outside of the technology field to join it. That group of prospective clients was the one we called "Career Changers."

Our corporate and government sales teams prospected into accounts to procure business, but that was not the case for our Career Changers team. For that team, we advertised in the employment section of the *Washington Post* Sunday Edition to generate inbound leads. The lead flow was entirely dependent on the placement of the ad in the newspaper. If it appeared above the fold, the ad performed extremely well and generated tons of leads for the Career Changers sales team. Sometimes, the *Washington Post* did not have advertising space available above the fold or even on the front page. When that happened, our lead volume for the week tanked.

For the weeks when our ad appeared somewhere other than above the fold, I dreaded coming into the office on Monday mornings. As I arrived, there was a line of salespeople at my door ready to complain about the poor ad placement and expected lead shortfall for the week. They were setting the stage for a poor selling week. They would say, "How am I supposed to hit my sales numbers when lead volume is down?"

While there was a large group of salespeople at my door, it did not include every member of the sales team. Maria and Tony were never in "the complaining group" and they were also my top performing salespeople. Think about that. My top salespeople never complained about lead volume and they continually crushed their sales numbers. Yet, their colleagues prepared me for their goal attainment shortfall, which of course was the company's fault, never theirs. Or so they claimed.

In contrast to the other salespeople on the team, Maria and Tony had a *different* perspective of the leads we generated. They viewed the *Washington Post* leads as the gravy for their sales. The meat, their primary lead source, was referrals. After the two of them had been selling for us for six months, they were completely self-sufficient. While their sales counterparts fretted over the placement of that week's ad, Maria and Tony built their business with a Referral *Sell Different!* strategy. And again, those two were, by far, my top performers.

Another interesting thing about Maria and Tony was their approach to working with their career changer clientele. Their counterparts saw the relationship as transactional. I shouldn't even describe their perception as a relationship because they simply looked to convert a lead into a sale. If and when that was accomplished, they moved on to the next lead, which the company (not they themselves) generated.

That was not the approach that Maria and Tony had with their clientele. They recognized that to be successful selling to Career Changers, they needed a Referral *Sell Different!* strategy. The selling approach required more than just a transaction. Someone who was exploring a career change and inquiring about our training programs experienced a myriad of worries. The cost to participate in these programs ranged between seven thousand and ten thousand dollars, and no loans or grants were available. The programs required a significant time commitment, and most career changers already had full-time jobs and families. Also, the training programs were tough. A fair number of Career Changers started training but didn't complete it because of either the time commitment or the program's rigor.

Maria and Tony understood career changer emotions and tailored their selling approach accordingly. They genuinely cared about the success of their clientele and didn't celebrate a sale until their client not only completed the training program, but had been hired into the technology industry. Because of the way they handled their clientele, referral leads poured in for them. While their sales counterparts may have sold a training program to an individual, Maria and Tony built a strong business by establishing valuable relationships with their clients.

The Business Developer's Mantra

While there are many takeaways from the Maria and Tony story, there is a huge one that I hope you recognize. If you see a lead as a potential sale, then you will, at most, have one sale. That's one of many reasons why I hate the word "closing." Closing implies it's the end of the process. There's nothing more to be done. If you see a lead as the beginning of a relationship, you can (and will) have multiple sales. Top salespeople embrace what I call "The Business Developer's Mantra."

Every deal must yield two more.

That mantra is a philosophical game changer for salespeople. It creates a compounding effect on your sales. Rather than thinking about winning a deal, top salespeople look at the award of a contract as the beginning of a potentially lucrative relationship. One of the ways that potential is recognized is through referrals. The "If You Were Me" strategy that I shared in the previous chapter is another application of The Business Developer's Mantra.

And why are referrals important? These leads convert to deals faster and at a higher rate than any other lead source. That's an irrefutable fact

If you see a lead as a potential sale, then you will, at most, have one sale.

that I'm sure you know. The primary reason why referral leads perform at those rates is trust. During the decision-making process, Decision Influencers attempt to validate the claims made by salespeople. Validation is much simpler for the DI when they were referred by a trusted source like a family member, friend, or colleague. IDC, a global marketing intelligence firm, found that 73 percent of executives prefer to work with salespeople referred by someone they know. Active referral lead generation is not a *nice-to-have* lead source. It's a *must-have*!

Have you ever thought about why people give referrals? It isn't just about what was sold to them, but also the experience they had when buying it. If the salesperson pushed and manipulated the DI to buy, it does not matter how good the product is, no referrals are coming his way. Not enough salespeople think about "the why" behind referrals. The experience a buyer has when purchasing has a direct impact on whether or not they will refer others to you.

The Business Developer's Mantra also helps salespeople avoid mixed emotions when winning a deal. They are excited to have the new account, but fearful because their sales pipeline is now barren. Top salespeople see deal wins as the tools they need to create more selling opportunities, not just winning a single deal.

A Question or a Campaign

There are two types of referral leads: passive and active. *Passive referral leads* are those generated without any effort from the company or the salesperson. A happy client passes along a salesperson's contact person to someone who expresses interest. That person contacts the salesperson to inquire about the products.

Active referral leads are generated through both company and salesperson initiatives. An active referral campaign means salespeople are soliciting this lead type. Not enough salespeople do this. When I ask salespeople about the referral leads they receive, most share stories of passive ones. It's a rarity when I hear of dedicated campaigns for active referrals. The old expression rings true: "If you don't ask, you don't get."

Think of getting referrals as a campaign, not merely an answer to a question. Top salespeople don't look at referral generation merely as a question to be asked and a box to be checked. They see it as their Referrals *Sell Different!* strategy, which is a lead generation campaign. Let's say that today, you ask a DI for a referral. She will share with you the information she knows today. Over the next several months, she will meet more people. Do you think she will remember your request for referrals? I bet she forgot about it minutes after you asked.

> Think of getting referrals as a campaign, not merely an answer to a question.

A referral campaign includes periodic requests for referrals. That begs the question of how often to ask someone for them. The answer is that it depends entirely on the relationship and frequency of communication you have. If you talk with a client every week and ask for a referral each time, that's a surefire way to tarnish the relationship. At most, the question should be asked once per quarter. How do you remember when you last asked and when to ask again? Referral campaign management is best handled by your CRM, as you can schedule tasks and document activities.

The One Time You Can Ask for Referrals

A favorite question of mine to ask salespeople is: When is the only time you can ask for referrals?

Some salespeople say it is appropriate when the contract is signed. Some say it is when the order is delivered. Others think it is post implementation. These are expected guesses, but they are all incorrect. There is one time, and only one time, in the entire relationship spectrum when it is appropriate to ask for referrals.

> **The one time when you can ask for a referral is when you have earned the right to do so.**

The timing of that "earned right" is different in each situation. There are instances when someone may never have spent a penny with you, but you provided tremendous value to them, and thus, earned the right to ask for referrals. I've also seen multi-year purchasing relationships in which the salesperson still has not earned the right to ask for referrals.

Salespeople have total control of "the when" when it comes to asking for referrals. If they are committed to providing value to DIs, beyond what their product offers, they can quickly shorten the timeline to achieve that earned right.

Requesting Referrals

While earning the right to ask for referrals is important, there also needs to be careful consideration of how to ask for them as well. Consider this:

Two elementary school classrooms are side by side with teachers presenting the same lesson to their respective groups of students. Each teacher presents the lesson equally proficiently and finishes at the same time.

At the end of the lesson, the first teacher looks over the top of her glasses and inquires, "Any questions?" Not one student raises a hand.

The teacher of the second class finishes the lesson, looks out at his students, and asks, "What questions can I answer for you?" He spends the next half hour fielding questions from his students.

Why am I sharing this anecdote with you? This story parallels a common salesperson approach when requesting referrals. Salespeople say some variation of, "Do you know of anyone who would be interested in what we offer?" The most common answer to that question is, "I can't think of anyone, but I'll call you if I come across someone who I think would be interested." Let me assure you. That phone call is not happening.

Leveraging Referrals *Sell Different!* strategy, make a subtle shift in how you request referrals. This shift will significantly change the number of active referral leads you generate. Ask for referrals this way:

> **"Given what you know about what we do, who do you know who would also be interested in what we offer?"**

"Who do you know" suggests that they know someone, even multiple people, who would be interested in what you sell. It's illogical to answer that question with a yes/no response based on how it is phrased. Try it. You'll be amazed by the impact a little shift in the way you ask for referrals can improve your active referral lead flow.

Before you ask for referrals, you also need to decide what you specifically want from the *referee*. "I want referrals," you may be thinking. Of course you want referrals! But how do you define a referral? Are you looking for just a name and an email address, or would you like for someone to facilitate an introduction? Top salespeople desire the latter. Receiving a name and email address sets you up for a lead that is only slightly warmer than a cold call.

To truly leverage the power of your Referrals *Sell Different!* strategy, you need the referring party to facilitate introductions for you. Once they share a referral name, ask them to send an email introducing you to that individual. That paves the way for you to initiate conversation with the referral. If they don't send the email within two days of agreeing to do so, send a reminder email and offer to write the introduction for them. Make it easy for them to introduce you.

■ ■ ■

Put Your Money Where Your Mouth Is

If you look at a business's profit and loss statement, you will often see line item expenses for lead generation, marketing, and business development. Rarely do I find companies making an investment in active referral lead generation. How does that make sense? As I said earlier, referrals turn into deals faster and at a higher rate than any other lead source. Why wouldn't there be dollars put toward that initiative? That's a head scratcher! DIRECTV had an entire ad campaign solely for its referral program. Clearly, they saw the value in driving the performance of this lead source.

If your company is not offering an incentive for referrals, I assure you that you are not maximizing what could be achieved from this lead source. To put that incentive program together, consider the sale amount you need to generate from the referral to justify compensation for the referring party. For example, you may determine that the referral needs to purchase a minimum of five thousand dollars of product to justify giving the *referee* a financial reward. Remember, there are lead generation costs from your other sales, so it should be easy to allocate dollars to drive the performance of your best lead source.

There are many ways you can structure compensation for those who refer you when the referrals result in won deals. As mentioned earlier, compensation should only be for those who facilitate introductions leading to sales. Only providing names and email addresses is not worthy of financial reward. With a little research, you could get that information on your own. If they are going to get something, they need to do something.

Here is an extremely effective referral compensation incentive. I call it the "favorite restaurant program." Let's say you determine you can allocate one hundred dollars for referrals that lead to a particular sale size. You would provide the referring parties a one-hundred-dollar gift certificate to their favorite restaurant based on their facilitating introductions to someone who ultimately buys at a specified amount. The reason this program has been so successful is that it personalizes the award. It also makes it more memorable. Here is how to share the program either on the phone or in person.

> **You:** Nicole, what is your favorite restaurant?
>
> **Nicole:** Harmon's.
>
> **You:** When was the last time you went there?
>
> **Nicole:** About six months ago.
>
> **You:** We would like to send you to Harmon's restaurant as our guest.
>
> **Nicole:** Really?
>
> **You:** Yes. Given our work together, I know you are very familiar with what we do and the quality of what we do. I'm sure you know many people in like roles in other companies. For each one you refer to us who spends $_____ or more, we will give you a one-hundred-dollar gift certificate to Harmon's restaurant.
>
> **Nicole:** Wow! That's cool.
>
> **You:** Who do you know that would also be interested in what we offer?
>
> **Nicole:** I know John Jones at XYX company has a new initiative and I believe this is something he would be interested in.
>
> **You:** Great. When can you send an email to John introducing me to him?

Beyond a dialogue like that, there is one other key step to take for your referral program to flourish. After verbally sharing the program, send an email explaining it. This serves as a reminder to the potential *referee*. For example:

> Thank you for allowing me to share our exciting referral program with you. As I mentioned, we want to send you to Harmon's restaurant as our guest. Every time you refer someone to us, and that person spends a minimum of $_____, you receive a one-hundred-dollar gift card to Harmon's restaurant.

Some companies have policies that prohibit their employees from receiving this type of compensation. If that is the case, then you can offer a donation to their company's favorite charity in the same amount as the "restaurant offer." For the charitable donation, be sure to talk with your financial team as there could be a tax benefit for your company, making this an even bigger win.

Industry Partner Referrals

I am often asked by salespeople how they can get industry salespeople with complementary or related offers to refer them to their clients. What won't work is calling them and just asking for referrals. Gimme! Gimme! Remember, if they had leads yesterday, they sent them to another salesperson. Why would they now send those leads to you? When I ask that question of salespeople, I usually hear a deafening silence, as they had not considered that point.

Industry salespeople can be a great source for active referral leads as part of your Referrals *Sell Different!* strategy. They can also be a great application of the "If You Were Me" strategy that I shared earlier. Often forgotten with this lead source is what I referenced earlier in this chapter: you have to earn the right to ask for them. Before you ask for leads, invest in those salespeople. Learn what they do and the types of clientele they seek. When they see you are interested in helping them, they will be more willing to help you.

As part of your active referral campaign, put together an incentive like the "favorite restaurant program." Invest in those salespeople and cultivate relationships by being genuinely interested in them and what they seek to accomplish. Then, and only then, will you have earned the right to ask for leads.

When you first started reading this chapter, you probably expected a basic overview of a sales task that you've heard about countless times. I hope you now see the opportunity to implement this Referrals *Sell Different!* strategy as well as have the tools to take advantage of this lead source to win more deals at the prices you want.

REFERRALS *SELL DIFFERENT!* CONCEPT

Passive referrals are provided based on product performance, but to generate active referrals, you need a thoughtful program and salespeople properly asking for them.

CHAPTER 5

HARNESSING THE POWER
OF VIRTUAL SELLING

O n March 12, 2020, I boarded a plane to Las Vegas with my wife, Sharon. We decided to turn my speaking engagement into a mini vacation for two.

At least that was our plan.

That evening, we attended a cocktail party hosted by my client. It was during that event that I saw the beginnings of the impact COVID-19 would have on business. For example, a few of the guests avoided shaking hands with one another. It was also the first time I heard the expression "social distancing" as guests conducted their conversations much farther apart than what was, at the time, considered normal.

The next morning, I delivered a keynote talk and workshop for the group. Overnight, more information about the virus had circulated. Steven, my son who plays baseball for Augsburg University, called and said his spring baseball trip to Arizona had been canceled. Both my daughter and younger son called to say their classes had been canceled for the rest of the semester. Rather than stay for our mini vacation, Sharon and I decided to fly home right after I delivered the program. You could feel change coming, but no one had any idea of the magnitude.

The virus gained traction and seemingly stopped the world from spinning. The number of people who would be afflicted, and die from it, was staggering. Business was brought to a screeching halt. Even the stock market was shut down for a period of time.

Selling Changed Because It Had To

One of the major business changes brought about by this pandemic was the forced shift to virtual selling. Because people did not want to meet in person, or because they were not permitted to, the only way to sell during this time was with a phone and/or a computer.

Virtual selling, which was seen by most people as new, created a lot of panic in the sales profession. However, it wasn't entirely new. Virtual selling was just inside sales "on steroids." The sales and sales management respect for the job inside salespeople performed reached new heights during this time. No longer was this job considered merely a junior-level sales role. Executives came to recognize that effective virtual selling required a specialized skill set and tools to deliver the desired results.

Virtual selling was just inside sales "on steroids."

Taking it a step further, a number of sales assessment tools highlight the point that someone who is effective at selling in person may not be as effective selling virtually. The converse is also true. Outside salespeople are accustomed to freedoms that virtual salespeople, which is what many outside salespeople became, do not have. For example, outside salespeople travel to appointments by car or plane, and have schedule flexibility that virtual salespeople do not.

Prospecting is challenging whether you are an inside or outside salesperson. Yet, virtual selling exposes the importance of voice inflection, diction, and tonality. For virtual sellers, voice is a key ingredient in their sales success recipe. Persona is so important that when I develop hiring processes for virtual salespeople, one of the interview steps is conducted virtually. During that interview, virtual selling persona is scrutinized as carefully as the candidate's answers. If a candidate cannot build a relationship in this interview, it is an indication that this person might not succeed in a virtual selling environment.

As in-person events came to a screeching halt, salespeople, accustomed to generating leads during in-person networking events, had to develop social media mastery, particularly on LinkedIn. The overall business development function, like the sales function, was forced to become virtual.

Outside salespeople were accustomed to conducting in-person meetings and having the advantage of observing the body language and facial expressions of their Decision Influencers. But with virtual selling, building relationships was different because salespeople weren't sitting in the same room with DIs. During an in-person meeting, when a DI was quiet, an outside salesperson could see them taking notes or leaning back in their chair to think, which led the salesperson to pause for a moment. With virtual selling, that opportunity is lost, unless you are using a webcam (a point I will come back to later in the chapter). Outside salespeople who were new to virtual selling didn't know how to handle the silence.

The same holds true with presentations. When presenting in person, salespeople have the opportunity to "read the room," but that isn't possible with virtual selling. Even with a webcam, it is much more challenging to analyze facial expressions and body language in group presentations. The images of the participants are small, and the salesperson's focus is on effectively facilitating the meeting.

When it comes to proposals, outside salespeople are used to sitting down in person with a DI and reviewing them. Virtual salespeople don't have that interaction, so they often email proposals and hope for a positive response.

There is also a perception that virtual selling is much more challenging than in-person selling. Some debate whether it can even be done. I'm here to tell you it can. Virtual selling is not harder; it's just different. To succeed, you need a Virtual Selling *Sell Different!* strategy.

Master Technology Before You Use It

Virtual selling exposed the need for several technology tools that were quickly introduced into the marketplace. Salespeople rushed to use these cool and exciting tools, which caused a big sales effectiveness problem. They rapidly implemented the tools into their virtual selling repertoire, but didn't invest time to master their use. Floundering with technology during a DI interaction detracts from the meeting and creates a negative impression. DIs don't blame your technology for not working properly. They blame you! Before you use any technology to sell, make sure you know how to use it properly.

> Floundering with technology during a DI interaction detracts from the meeting and creates a negative impression.

Always test the technology prior to every DI meeting. Hardware and software updates can sometimes cause issues with other applications. You don't want to be surprised by a technology snafu as you begin your meeting.

For sales managers, I encourage you to test your salespeople's proficiency on every technology before they can use it when selling. Put together a simulation exercise that allows your salespeople to demonstrate that they can use the tool. It is best to have them demonstrate proficiency in a test environment rather than burn a DI relationship because they didn't know how to use it properly.

Webcam or Not?

One of the first technology decisions you have to make is the use of a webcam when selling. Some executives and salespeople feel it is a must for virtual selling. Others feel it is an unnecessary distraction.

Using a webcam provides an important benefit, which is the ability to see the DI's facial expressions and some of their body language. It somewhat mimics an in-person sales interaction. That's my argument for using webcams when it is appropriate. Ah . . . but what does "appropriate" mean?

There are considerations for both the salesperson and the DI if a webcam is to be used. First, the salesperson has to be mindful of their appearance. Sloppy attire or a messy background can be an immediate turnoff. If you are going to use a webcam, be careful of how you dress and the background the DI will see. It will affect the DI's impression of you, your company, and what you're selling, which means it will affect your deal.

Just like you gain the advantage of seeing their facial expressions and body language, your DI sees yours. That can be an advantage or a disadvantage. For one, because the way many office chairs are designed, many salespeople have poor desk posture. They sit slumped in their chairs, which can create a negative impression on camera. Some salespeople fidget or play with their pens while on a call. Worst of all, some salespeople text and email during the virtual meeting. They see you doing all these things, which again creates a negative impression of you! If you are caught multitasking on your webcam, your deal will be dead. That means if you are going to use a webcam, you need to be highly sensitive to your screen persona.

Using a webcam is different from meeting in person. We are accustomed to looking people in the eye. That's what we all have been trained to do. With a webcam, we see the DIs on our computer screen. Looking into their eyes is not truly looking into their eyes in this case. We need to look into the lens of our camera to actually be looking into their eyes. It takes a while to get comfortable doing that. Plus, laptop computer webcams cause you to look down when staring into the camera. So, elevate the laptop by placing a stack of books under it, so you are looking straight ahead. All of this means you need preparation and practice using a webcam on your own before you use it when selling.

When using webcams, and any other technology when virtual selling, provide DIs with clear, step-by-step meeting setup instructions. You'll find some DIs are very comfortable with technology while others are not. Plus, competing virtual meeting technologies have nuances when using them and your DI could get frustrated trying to figure them out. When providing DIs with meeting information and instructions, include your phone number so they can call you if they have any difficulties joining the meeting. Those difficulties might not have anything to do with the technology; it could be that their internal firewall is blocking them from joining the meeting.

Here's another reason to use webcams whenever possible: if you can see them, they are much less likely to put their phone on mute and multitask. Trust me, it happens! For obvious reasons, we don't want them conducting side conversations or reading emails as we are sharing important information.

Now that I have presented my case for using a webcam, it probably reads like it is a no-brainer. "We should do it for every virtual sales call." Hang on! There is another aspect to consider before you turn that camera on. You need to think about the other person in the virtual meeting. He may not want to be seen, particularly if he works from home and doesn't feel "camera friendly" that day. Or, if he works in an office and has proprietary information on a whiteboard or a messy desk, he might not want to have a video call. The key is to offer your DI the opportunity for a video call, but don't assume he wants to have that type of interaction with you. Asking, rather than assuming, helps avoid an uncomfortable situation.

You also have the option of having your webcam on while theirs is off. That way they see you, but you don't see them. It's not the best option, but it is better than no webcam at all.

Making a Great First Impression

One of our goals for a virtual meeting is to create a great first impression with our DI. One way to do that is to propose an agenda in the invitation and ask for their feedback. Notice the use of the word "propose" rather than "set."

In the invitation, propose an agenda by saying something like:

> **"What I was planning to cover during our meeting is A, B, and C. For this to be a great use of your time, what is it you want to be sure we talk about?"**

The answer to that question helps gain clarity on what is most important to your DI and what should be accomplished during the meeting. By proposing an agenda, you communicate that you are interested in what they want to achieve during the meeting, not just what you want to cover.

On meeting day, always arrive ten minutes prior to the start of the meeting. This gives you time to make sure the technology is working properly. Turn off your cell phone. Place an "in virtual meeting" sign outside your office or cubicle. If you work from home, place a sign over your doorbell. All of these steps help to avoid unnecessary interruptions.

At the beginning of every virtual meeting using a webcam, start by making sure you can see and hear one another. This is an additional way to avoid awkward encounters. Be sure to close unnecessary applications so they don't impede meeting-software performance.

While it is convenient to use the audio functions in your PC, use your phone instead. You'll find your phone's audio quality to be superior to what your PC produces. But never use a speakerphone. Many people find it disrespectful. It sounds distant, the audio breaks up, and it can come across as arrogant. Use a headset so that you have the best audio experience possible. And encourage your DIs to use a phone for the audio portion of the meeting so they have a great experience as well.

Another way to make a great first impression is to create a welcome page using PowerPoint. Include their name, logo, and topics you proposed for the agenda. Share your screen when you arrive so they immediately see the welcome page. Accessing most virtual meeting technologies requires multiple steps. It almost feels like you are entering codes to launch nuclear missiles. Even with all those steps, DIs still aren't sure they are in the right virtual room. Personalization sets the stage for a great meeting.

Another benefit of virtual meetings is the opportunity to record them. Prior to hitting the "record" button at the beginning of the meeting, be sure to ask your DI for permission to do so. Don't be surprised if they ask you to email them a copy of the recording as this allows them to focus on the conversation during the meeting rather than on note-taking.

The Virtual Selling Process

Building rapport is something we all have been taught to do. When we meet a DI in person, we may make small talk about the weather, last night's ballgame, or something of interest we see in their office. The expectation in a virtual selling environment is different. DIs expect you to be much more sensitive to their time and begin business conversations more quickly. Use the business conversation to build rapport rather than what might be perceived as wasting time chitchatting.

Conducting discovery conversations virtually isn't much different from an in-person meeting. Prior to the virtual discovery meeting, identify your criteria for success, formulate the questions you will ask, and prepare the information you will share. Again, this preparation exercise is no different than when the meeting is conducted in person.

During the virtual meeting, talk more slowly than you normally would during an in-person meeting. If you talk quickly, your DI may miss key information. And if you ever have an uncomfortable situation where you are both talking at the same time, always let them speak first. After all, we want them talking more than we do. What they have to say is more important to the sale than what you have to say at that moment.

As I suggested earlier, effective virtual selling requires you to be comfortable with DI silence during the meeting. They may be thinking or taking notes. Disrupting those activities can cause your DI to lose their train of thought, which detracts from the sale. An effective virtual selling strategy is, at the beginning of the meeting, to ask the DI to share with you when they are taking notes so you can pause. Plus, you should plan pauses after important sections of the conversation. Tell them you are pausing to allow for note-taking, and ask them to let you know when to move on.

During the virtual presentation stage of the process, there is a common mistake salespeople make with their visuals: too many words or an overly complicated, hard-to-follow graphic image on the screen. This can be fatal for your deal.

If this sounds like your approach and you bristled, allow me to explain why that is a major issue. *People cannot read and listen effectively simultaneously.* It doesn't work! Try it. You'll quickly experience the problem. That means the more words placed on the slide, the less the DI is listening to what you have to say. Since one of the goals during a presentation is engagement with the participants, that visual approach creates an avoidable barrier. Effective presentations are conversations, not soliloquies. What is shown on-screen should foster conversation, not hinder it.

The primary reason salespeople have so much text on slides is not for the DI's benefit, but rather their own. They are unprepared for the meeting. They use the visual of the slide to tell them what to say or they read it verbatim. That is an awful reason to clutter the visual portion of your presentation. Instead, use a "notes" function that the DI won't see, and master your delivery.

The word "presentation" conveys the wrong message to salespeople. When DIs ask for presentations, salespeople think the request is for a forty-five-minute lecture with a fifteen-minute question-and-answer period. The word "presentation" may come up, but a DI is looking for something else. Rather than concern yourself with just the content on the slide, introspectively ask how to turn the presentation into a conversation. I assure you if you are talking longer than five consecutive minutes, they are not listening to you. You've lost their attention. You will have delivered a masterful soliloquy about your company and its solutions. But no one heard it.

Here's a simple tip for the visual portion of your presentation. If DIs can have the same experience reading the slides on their own, what was the point of the virtual presentation meeting? There was none. Use visual text for emphasis of discussion points, not to read to the participants. For each slide, develop questions to create DI engagement. This will prevent you from lecturing throughout the entire meeting.

Use visual text for emphasis of discussion points, not to read to the participants.

Any time words are necessary on the slides, use a "build" function so that meeting participants only see the relevant text for that part of the discussion. And there is no law that says text must be preceded by bullet points. In most cases, having a single word/phrase or a graphic on-screen is more powerful than having multiple bullet points. (If you are thinking these issues are not limited to virtual selling, you are correct. This is a significant issue with in-person presentations as well.)

Some salespeople try to use their virtual presentations to serve two purposes: to facilitate the meeting and as a tool to send to the DI afterward, as a reminder of the content. Rather than trying to serve a dual purpose, use two tools. Use the presentation strictly as a tool to facilitate your meeting. Then provide the DI with a narrative summary of the meeting highlights. (I explain the structure of the narrative email in chapter 11.) This helps to ensure both tools are effective in helping you win the deal at the prices you want.

Afterward, provide the DI with a narrative summary of the meeting highlights. This helps to ensure both tools are effective in helping you win the deal at the prices you want.

When it comes time to document the solution in a proposal, many virtual salespeople email it to the DI and hope for the best. Ouch! DIs read the proposal by flipping to the pricing page and, if they don't like what they see, go dark on you, never to be heard from again. A proposal should be presented in a virtual meeting and never emailed to the DI until after that meeting has been held. This gives the DI the opportunity to ask questions as you guide them through the sections of the proposal and for you to receive feedback. Emailing the proposal without that virtual meeting can lead to a sales black hole and you'll never hear from the DI again. Before you hit the "send" button, make sure you understand the next steps of their decision-making process or you will be left wondering about the status of your deal.

One final point about virtual selling. Remember to smile during the meetings. That's important whether you are using a webcam or not. Smiling changes tonality in your voice. DIs can "hear you smiling" even when they can't see your face. While the words you say are important, how they are said is also important. If smiling on the phone is not something you are accustomed to doing, place a mirror in front of you so that you can see your countenance during virtual meetings. That subtle change can have a major impact on the virtual conversations you have with DIs.

Virtual selling began as a necessity, but it quickly became recognized as a *Sell Different!* opportunity. It has been proven to increase sales productivity by eliminating travel, which also reduces the cost of sale. During the pandemic, executives and salespeople realized that they could win deals at the prices they want through effective virtual selling. Top sales forces analyzed conversion metrics during each phase of the new client acquisition process and made adjustments to increase effectiveness. Adjust the process, master the technology, and take advantage of this great selling opportunity because virtual selling is here to stay.

To download my Virtual Selling Best Practices eBook, visit www.VirtualSellingBestPractices.com

VIRTUAL SELLING *SELL DIFFERENT!* CONCEPT

New client acquisition process accommodations and technology mastery are the keys to virtual selling success.

CHAPTER 6

THE CRITICAL PERSON NEEDED TO WIN MORE DEALS AT THE PRICES YOU WANT

W hen I was growing up in New York City, I wasn't a big fan of reading. Other than the sports pages in the *New York Post* and *New York Daily News*, the only reading interest I had was Encyclopedia Brown books. I loved trying to solve the mysteries along with Leroy Brown (aka Encyclopedia Brown—Everyone's Favorite Boy Detective). I would even reread sections in search of clues, hoping to solve the mysteries before the author revealed the culprits.

As an adult, I still don't love reading, much to the chagrin of my mother, a former New York City public school teacher. While I don't read for enjoyment, I constantly read to grow in my profession, and I love television mysteries, especially *Law & Order* (only the original version). I can't tell you how many times I've watched all 456 episodes. Watching *Law & Order* is also one of the fond memories I have of when Sharon and I were first dating. I'd go to her apartment on Wednesday nights and we would watch the first-run episodes. Just like with Encyclopedia Brown books, I tried to solve the mysteries before the perpetrators were exposed.

My interest in solving mysteries is a strategy I applied to sales to make it both fun and effective. I've always looked at selling not as peddling wares, but rather trying to solve a Decision Influencer "mystery." I had to search for clues to solve it. The people involved in the decision-making process had challenges and goals. The mystery I had to solve was discovering what those challenges and goals were and crafting a solution that the DIs would be excited to buy.

Just as I did with the mystery books and television shows, I had to analyze each person I encountered. That meant figuring out the motivators for a DI to act on what I had to offer and determining their ability to effect change in their organization. I tried to determine which DIs were most supportive of my solution and which were the most heavily influential in the decision-making process. In essence, I searched for a Decision Influencer entity I refer to as a "Mentor" and used a Mentor *Sell Different!* strategy.

You've probably heard the sales term "internal coach" or "champion," but I always felt those expressions were vague. To qualify as a Mentor, there are two specific criteria: passion about what your company offers and a strong influence in the decision-making process.

Mentor Ranking

Potential Mentors are ranked using two scales. Each scale has a zero to five ranking. The first scale measures *Level of Commitment* to your solution. This DI is someone who passionately believes what you offer is the right solution for their needs. The higher the commitment, the higher the score. Here are the criteria salespeople need to consider when scoring a DI's *Level of Commitment*:

- What would a solution need to include and address for this DI to support it?
- How does the discussed solution compare with what the DI currently has or is considering?
- What are the meaningful differences between my solution and the alternatives?

- Why do those differences matter specifically to this DI?
- Are those differences significant enough for the DI to take action?
- When does the DI want this solution implemented?
- Why is that date significant to the DI and to the organization?
- What are the consequences of that date not being met?
- What could their current provider do that would result in the DI deciding not to support a change?
- If the competition offered a price 15 percent lower than mine, would this DI still be firmly entrenched in support of my solution?

Failure to consider the impact of price (highlighted in the final question) is a common mistake when evaluating DI commitment. Will the DI buckle? Some are committed to a solution solely because they feel they are receiving the best price (not the best value) from a provider. But then a competitor arrives on the scene, offers a lower price, and gains the DI's loyalty.

> Some are committed to a solution solely because they feel they are receiving the best price (not the best value) from a provider.

The second scale measures *Level of Influence* in the decision-making process. Scrutiny of influence is also tricky. Some DIs position themselves as the be all, end all in the decision-making process. Others assure you that their boss will "rubber stamp" their approval of the deal. In my experience, it is rare to find a true "rubber stamp" situation. "Rubber stamp" is most often a smoke screen that fools salespeople into thinking the status of their deal is higher than it is.

Here are the criteria to consider when scoring a DI's *Level of Influence*:

- What needs to happen for the DI's recommendation (my solution) to be selected?
- When this DI makes recommendations to the company, what normally happens?

- Who else should be involved in the selection process going forward?
- What thoughts and perspectives will they have about the DI's recommendation?
- Why would they not support the selection of this solution?
- If they don't support the DI's recommendation, what happens to the deal?
- Does this DI have enough clout in the organization to effect change?

Similar to the *Level of Commitment* scale, the higher the level of decision-making influence the DI has, the higher the score. The seven questions provide you with insight to analyze the level of decision-making authority the DI possesses in this particular deal.

Level of Influence is a tricky evaluation. You may be dealing with a senior executive who has the authority to award you the deal but won't do it without the support of her direct reports. Or, you may be working with a DI who needs senior-level approval to award you the deal. In both instances, strategy is needed to advance your deal.

Deal Vulnerabilities

As you meet DIs during your account pursuits, rank each one using the two scales and add the scores together. Sales utopia is a DI with a combined score of ten, but that is extremely rare to find. The challenge salespeople face when implementing the Mentor-ranking strategy is that it requires self-honesty. Salespeople are naturally optimistic. That's one of the aspects that always attracted me to the profession. I love being around positive people. However, there are times when optimism creates blind spots in your deal. I'm not suggesting you become a pessimist, but rather adopt the pragmatist philosophy. A Mentor who ranks as a five in both categories will rarely, if ever, emerge. In those instances, rather than feel confident about the deal, ask yourself the converse:

What might prevent the deal from happening?

Answering that question honestly exposes deal risks for action to be taken. When in doubt, rank lower on the scale. With that approach, you will avoid the risk of being overly optimistic and overlooking deal vulnerabilities. A Mentor with a perfect score happens for one of two reasons: either it's an anomaly or the salesperson was not self-honest.

Any score less than a five, in either scale, means the deal has vulnerabilities. Is the DI not demonstrating firm commitment to your solution being selected? Does an influential DI have a personal relationship with the incumbent? Has a new DI entered the picture? Is there a political battle inside the organization? To be successful winning deals at the prices you want, carefully evaluate each potential Mentor, identify the weaknesses in your deal, and develop strategies to eliminate them.

With *Level of Commitment* deal vulnerabilities, the strategy to resolve scores of less than five is to effectively differentiate both *what you sell* and *how you sell* to demonstrate meaningful value. Consider whether or not the DI you are interacting with can become passionate about the solutions you offer. If not, then continue your search for the right Mentor candidate. If they have the potential to be excited about the solution, the burden is on the salesperson to arouse that excitement.

> If you are to win deals at the prices you want, a strong Mentor is needed every time.

With *Level of Influence* deal vulnerabilities, the requisite strategy is to find a more influential DI because the deal could collapse without having that person in your camp.

When I think about my personal sales, my sales teams' sales, and my consulting clients' sales, one constant theme comes to the forefront: if you are to win deals at the prices you want, a strong Mentor is needed every time.

Think about the deals you have won and lost. With the deals you won at the prices you wanted, you most likely had a heavily influential DI as a Mentor. When you lost or had to lower your prices to win the deal, you probably didn't have strong enough relationships with the most influential DIs. Sales is often seen as complicated, but identifying the right Mentor for each deal simplifies the entire account pursuit strategy. The search for the right Mentor for the deal serves as the core focus for your selling approach.

The Wizard

Sales would be pure bliss if you had the opportunity to engage the ultimate decision maker directly. I call this DI the "Wizard," an Oz-like decision maker who desires to remain hidden. In sales, the Wizard is the DI who signs the contract for your deal. This DI is sometimes masterful at staying behind the curtain and refusing to engage with you directly.

If that DI is not directly involved in the decision-making process, the deal has vulnerabilities that can be eliminated by a strong Mentor who can sell internally. Actually, the needed Mentor isn't just someone who *can* sell internally, but will fight for your solution to be adopted because he believes it is the right one.

Potential Mentor Pitfalls

To solve your sales mystery, the quest is to find the right potential Mentor candidates. Who in the organization will be most intrigued by what you have to offer? If the primary benefit of what you sell is cost reduction, DIs who are focused on that issue are great Mentor candidates. Same holds true for every benefit of what you sell. Pursue those DIs whose interests are most aligned with the benefits of what you sell. When you find DIs who are passionate about those aspects, consider them for

Mentor roles. However, don't forget the *Level of Influence* scale in the Mentor selection process.

It is possible to have a DI who is passionate about your solution, but lacks the authority to drive change in the organization. This means your deal fails. DIs with high *Level of Commitment* scores, but low *Level of Influence* scores, make for weak Mentors.

I'll share an example of this issue in my world. Sometimes, regional sales managers contact me regarding sales compensation concerns. They want to make changes to the company's compensation plan that is currently in place for salespeople. They feel the current compensation approach is flawed and they are passionate about the need to make a change. But they cannot contract with me to help them resolve that issue. Why? Because someone higher in the organization owns sales compensation. Without that DI involved, I would be wasting my sales time on a deal that is highly unlikely to happen. The same holds true for you when it comes to investing your time. DIs with high *Level of Commitment* scores, but low *Level of Influence* scores, create sales mirages that fool salespeople into believing their deals are stronger than they actually are.

What about a DI who is very friendly toward you? Is that an indication that this person can be a strong Mentor? Nope. Don't use DI friendliness as part of your Mentor evaluation. That has no bearing on the two Mentor scales. Some people are just fundamentally friendly, but they aren't passionate about the issues you address. Others may be curmudgeons who nonetheless see the value in what you offer and have the authority to make change happen. DI personality is not a consideration when scoring a Mentor.

While it is nice to have support from a DI, if this person does not have significant clout in his organization, he will not be able to perform the necessary role of the Mentor. The *Level of Influence* that the Mentor has within the organization is key to your deal's success. Since the Mentor is the internal seller, it is critical that this DI be heavily influential in the decision-making process to win the deal at the prices you want.

The Monster Mentor

A number of years ago, I was hired as Vice President of Sales and Marketing for a company. I reported directly to the CEO who was also an owner of the company. Before I ever went to him with an idea that I wanted to pursue, I did my homework and prepared for the meeting. Yet, I rarely was successful in those meetings.

I would come into the meetings and tell the CEO exactly what I wanted to do. I was looking for his rubber stamp to proceed. For all the questions he asked, I had thoughtful responses. But I wasn't able to get the green light I wanted.

One day, while I was in the shower thinking about this struggle, the answer hit me like a ton of bricks. I was going into these meetings looking for his stamp of approval, which meant my approach was flawed. I was telling him what I wanted to do but not asking for his perspective on the idea. He was both a CEO and an owner and it never dawned on me to ask for his input. Because of my flawed approach, rather than agree to the idea, he would rebuff it or put it off. From a sales perspective, I couldn't get my deals done because of my selling approach.

Based on this epiphany, I changed the way I sold my ideas. I still performed all the research I did prior, but I didn't come in looking for an easy "yes." Whenever I had an idea to run past him, I had to sell him on it. I started each meeting by saying, "I was thinking about doing this. What are your thoughts?" After I made this change in my approach, I came out of most of our meetings with the affirmative responses I sought.

Mentors commonly make the same mistake that I did. During your interactions with a DI, you arouse tremendous passion for your solution, which leads to a high ranking on the *Level of Commitment* scale. Thus, they become a Mentor. This Mentor is so excited that she is willing to run through walls for the solution to be selected. Sometimes, this energy causes fatal flaws in your deal. Typically, the Mentor is not a professional salesperson and does not know how to sell the organization on her ideas. The Mentor needs your counsel on selling, so there is not irreparable damage in the decision-making process.

Salespeople need to coach their Mentors on strategies to sell the deal. The Mentor is excited about the solution presented by the salesperson and feels strongly that it is the right solution for the company. The salesperson's job is to help the Mentor get what the Mentor wants. If the Mentor gets what she wants, then the salesperson gets the deal at the prices he wants. If the salesperson is merely trying to sell the deal to get a fat commission check, the Mentor strategy fails, and the deal is lost.

Earlier in the chapter, I presented the Wizard, who is the ultimate decision maker for your deal. There is another DI role of which to be mindful and it is not a pleasant one. This DI is the "Saboteur" who prefers either the status quo or an alternative solution.

Salespeople and their Mentors sometimes unknowingly create deal Saboteurs. Let's say there is a DI who has not been asked to be part of the solution development process. That alone can create a deal Saboteur. It's basic human psychology. When people feel left out of decision-making, they rebuff the decision made by others. Had they been asked to be involved, they would now likely support the solution that they oppose. When DIs are left out of the decision-making process, you are, in essence, inviting them to explore alternatives with your competitors whose solutions these Saboteur DIs will readily support. Why? Because they were involved.

You now know of a potential misstep in your deal, but your Mentor might not see the cliff she is about to go over. That means you need to coach your Mentor when you see this type of situation unfolding.

Consider this potential conversation:

> "Mary, I want to thank you for your support of the solution we have developed. I've been thinking about our approach and have some concerns. May I share them with you?" (Once accepted, continue.)

"I've worked with executives like you for a long time. At this point of the process, they pursue one of two paths. If I can take a moment to describe these two . . ." (Once accepted, continue.)

"One path is to engage all the key members of the decision-making team and solicit their input in the development of the solution. This makes everyone feel included, and once the final solution is created, they are all supportive of it. They all get the solution they want. These are the solutions that work best because the key stakeholders feel they had an opportunity to be heard.

"The other path is the one whereby one person works directly with me without any team involvement. We develop a solution that we feel everyone will support. Once the solution is developed, the team is told about it. What typically happens in this case is that this person does not receive accolades for a job well done. Instead, she is greeted by resistance and skepticism for no reason other than the fact that these people feel they were left out of the process.

"This is what causes some concern. I may be wrong, but it feels like we are going down the latter path. I feel obligated to share this with you but am not sure of the best way to proceed. I am looking to you for guidance. What should we do?"

This tactic communicates a core message. You aren't trying to sell her something. You are guiding her down a path to help her get what she wants. This approach communicates a message of support to the Mentor. She will recognize that the salesperson has her best interests in mind. This conversation also helps you to be seen as a trusted advisor. The Mentor's commitment to you and your solution is elevated (*Level of Commitment*), as she knows you genuinely care about her, not her wallet.

You will also notice that, while you know the path to select, you aren't lecturing the Mentor. You are guiding her to see the potential issues in the approach and leading her to make the choice that ensures she gets what she wants.

The Big Question Your Mentor Must Be Able to Answer

Through Mentor development, your DI firmly believes what you offer is the right solution for the company. In most cases, your Mentor has to sell others in the organization on the idea. Again, most Mentors are not salespeople, which means you need to help her get what she wants.

The first question other DIs will ask her is:

> **"Why is this solution your recommendation?"**

This question will be asked of colleague DIs and the Wizard as well. If your Mentor does not have a crisp and clear response to this question, the deal is in jeopardy and Saboteurs could be created.

Many salespeople perform the "happy dance" when they feel they have a Mentor who will fight to get the deal done and are later disappointed when the deal falls apart. This disappointment can be avoided by asking a simple question:

> **"I appreciate that ours is the solution you are recommending for your company. May I ask why we are your recommendation?"**

The answer to that question is telling. Oftentimes, you will find that your Mentor supports your solution for a specific reason or two. Yet, there are other reasons that may be important to her fellow DIs. Based on her response to that question, remind her of the other reasons (differentiators) that could resonate with the other DIs. Most important, offer to send her an email with speaking points to arm her with the information she will need to execute this critical sales function.

Whether or not the Mentor is also the Wizard, it is important that the Mentor be able to describe the specific reasons for supporting your solution. You are relying on the Mentor *selling* the plan to other DIs. Mentors who are also Wizards need to sell their subordinates on the decision. Non-Wizard Mentors need to sell their colleagues and superiors. It is the salesperson's responsibility to prepare the Mentor to sell the solution within the organization. Remember, you are asking a non-salesperson to sell for you, which means the burden of preparing the Mentor for success is entirely on your shoulders.

The reason this component of the Mentor *Sell Different!* strategy is crucial to your sales success is credibility. In most cases, internal people have more credibility in their organization than salespeople. These people are seen as looking out for the best interests of the company, not trying to earn the biggest commission check possible. Consequently, the Mentor's perspective is seen as more credible since she has nothing to gain by leading the company astray.

Dealing with Committees

In many organizations, buying decisions are made by committee. This makes having a strong Mentor even more important. You need someone on the inside fighting for your solution.

> Salespeople have a responsibility to help the Mentor see potential deal speed bumps and develop strategies to avoid them.

Often, when we hear the word "committee," we imagine a structured group with aligned objectives and a clear method to make a decision. That is rarely the case. It's usually a loosely formed group, some with their own agendas, and an unclear decision-making process.

When you have a Mentor with a high *Level of Commitment* ranking, the task at hand is to help her get what she wants. Salespeople have a responsibility to help the Mentor see potential deal speed bumps and develop strategies to avoid them. Without doing this, those speed bumps can become deal-killing brick walls.

Here are a series of questions to help you analyze the committee dynamic, so you can guide your Mentor to get what she wants:

- How many people are involved in the evaluation process?
- How were those people selected to participate in the evaluation process?
- What departments are represented in the evaluation group?
- What role do you play in the evaluation group?
- What are the evaluation group's main objectives?
- How does the solution we discussed fit with their main objectives?
- What involvement did this group have with selecting the current solution?
- What thoughts will they have about your recommendation?
- What can I provide for you that will help your colleagues see what you see in our solution?
- Why would they not support our solution being adopted?
- If any of them don't support your recommendation, what happens next?
- How will the group make a decision?

The answers to these questions are very telling relative to the strength of your deal. You will certainly have a clearer picture of your Mentor's *Level of Influence* ranking.

If you were to conduct an analysis of the deals you won, you would find:

- The most profitable deals and happiest clients had strong Mentors in place.
- Deals without a Mentor (or a weak one) were typically awarded based on low price.

When reviewing deal losses, one of the following statements is likely true:

- The deal lacked a strong, well-developed, and well-coached Mentor.
- A low-ranking Mentor was too weak to make the deal happen.

Be like Encyclopedia Brown. Place your detective magnifying glass on each DI. Search for and coach the right DI with the potential to become the strong Mentor you need to win the deal at the prices you want.

MENTOR *SELL DIFFERENT!* CONCEPT

To win more deals at the prices you want, a well-coached Mentor who is firmly committed to your solution and is heavily influential in decision-making is essential.

CHAPTER 7

THE MYTH OF CLOSING PROBLEMS

I n chapter 6, I shared my passion for solving mysteries. I applied that love to sales through the search for the right Mentor to help me win more deals at the prices I wanted. There is another way that I incorporate mystery solving into sales: through the discovery phase of the new client acquisition process.

On a regular basis, executives reach out to me because they believe their salespeople have a major problem that is killing their business. What is the problem? Closing! "My salespeople can't close," they say. (As mentioned in an earlier chapter, I despise the use of the word "close." Deals come to fruition. They are not closed. But I use "close" in this chapter because it is ubiquitous in sales.)

I always respond by asking what they mean. "Are they unable to ask for the order?"

"No, that's not the problem," they say.

"What then is the closing problem you are experiencing?" I ask.

That's when the floodgates open.

"My salespeople tell me about deals they are pursuing and how confident they feel about winning them. Then, they get to the final stage of the new client acquisition process and the deals unravel. Some Decision Influencers stop responding to them. Others develop a litany of concerns, objections, and stalls as the deals go nowhere. For the deals we are able to win, we have to drop prices to unacceptable levels. All of that can be summed up as, 'We have a closing problem.'"

After hearing this, I thank the executives for sharing this information with me and proceed to disagree with their assessment of the problem. "Based on what you shared with me, you don't have a 'closing' problem," I tell them. "'Closing' is a symptom of the actual issue you are experiencing."

Puzzled by my response, they ask, "What is the *actual* issue my salespeople have?"

This leads to a lengthy conversation about a foundational issue across the sales profession. The root cause isn't at the finish line. It's not about winning the deal. Rather, the problem resides at the starting line, at their handling of the discovery phase of the new client acquisition process. A Discovery *Sell Different!* strategy is the solution to this problem.

Some companies and salespeople use the expression "discovery" with their DIs. "We are going to have a discovery meeting." *Ouch!* Discovery is a sales expression. It is for our internal strategy development and should never be used with DIs. Here's why. When a DI hears you use the expression "discovery," she assumes she is about to go through a sales process. Immediately, she becomes guarded and defensive. After all, who looks forward to going through a sales process? If you have been using that expression, consider an alternative expression such as "consultation." Salespeople should use words and phrases that communicate value and benefit to the DI, rather than using their own jargon.

Forgetting What You Already Knew

One of the most accepted sales premises is that people buy based on emotion and justify their decisions with logic. Just about every salesperson on the planet, at one time or another, has heard that expression. Yet, many salespeople don't apply that concept when selling, particularly in the discovery phase of the new client acquisition process.

In my work developing discovery strategies with clients, I find their emphasis is on acquiring data and sharing information. As they think through the discovery process, they approach it entirely from a logical perspective. That approach isn't wrong, but it is incomplete.

Emotion drives DI action, not logic. How many times have you presented a strong business case to a DI, but he never acted on it? We all have had those experiences. The logical case to act was strong and valid, but the deal never moved forward. The missing step was arousing the DI's emotions to a level that would get him to take action on the proposed solution.

Emotion drives DI action, not logic.

Regardless of what you sell, DIs feel a certain way about their situation before you meet with them. I'll use an example that's easy to understand: a vacuum cleaner. By the time you meet with DIs for a discovery meeting about vacuum cleaners, they have already experienced emotions that led them to meet with you. Examples include *frustration* about the cleanliness of their carpeting, *irritation* about their current vacuum cleaner continually breaking, and *worry* about a family member in their home with allergies. It is those emotions that led them to accept a meeting with you to talk about a new vacuum cleaner. That means there is an important question salespeople need to ask themselves:

> **How do I expect Decision Influencers to feel about the challenges I address prior to meeting with me?**

Once salespeople have an understanding of DI pre-meeting emotions, the next step is another important introspective question:

> **How do I want Decision Influencers to feel after my meeting with them?**

Salespeople may understand how DIs feel pre-meeting, but don't necessarily determine how they want DIs to feel post-meeting. Without answering that question, how can you possibly guide the DI through an emotional transformation that leads to action? You can't and won't. Worst of all, there is a high risk of your deal stalling out.

To incorporate this component into your discovery strategy, make a list of all the potential states of mind that a DI may be experiencing prior to meeting with you. For each one, ask yourself why they feel the way they do. Here is a master list of common potential DI emotions and feelings:

- Accountable
- Afraid
- Angry
- Anxious
- Behind
- Competitive
- Complacent
- Concerned
- Confident
- Confused
- Creative
- Defeated
- Disappointed
- Disrespected
- Empowered
- Energized

- Envious
- Euphoric
- Excited
- Exposed
- Fearful
- Frustrated
- Happy
- Informed
- Inspired
- Interested
- Intrigued
- Invested
- Nervous
- Optimistic
- Overconfident
- Overwhelmed

- Pessimistic
- Responsible
- Sad
- Satisfied
- Scared
- Skeptical
- Supported
- Sympathetic
- Terrified
- Timid
- Triumphant
- Understanding
- Unempowered
- Uninformed
- Unsupported
- Worried

After you develop this list, make another list of the states of mind you want them to experience after meeting with you. Again, for each one you identify, ask yourself why you expect them to feel that way post-meeting. In the example with the vacuum cleaner, you might want the DI to feel *confident* they found a reliable vacuum cleaner that removes allergens from their carpeting.

Identifying the start and end points for their emotions was the easy part of discovery strategy development. The tough part is developing the plan to transform their emotions from what they felt before the meeting to how you want them to feel afterward. Here are some techniques to guide emotional transformation during discovery:

- Ask questions to help them emotionally evaluate the situation they are in and recognize the opportunities a new solution provides.
- Share information that arouses emotion like client success stories whereby the client had the same concerns that this DI presently has.
- Show pictures, charts, and graphs to emphasize important message points. Remember, a large percentage of the population is comprised of visual learners, which necessitates using illustrations to create an emotional stir.
- If applicable, demonstrate the solution in action either live or on video. In the vacuum cleaner example, show it in action.

If you aren't winning deals at the prices you want, evaluate the emotional aspects of your discovery process. If emotional transformation is not a key part of your discovery strategy, that may be the reason why your deals don't come to fruition.

Dental Discovery

Emotions drive DI action, but logic is important as well because DIs use it to justify their decisions. Another common reason why weak discovery is the root cause of perceived closing issues is the approach to DI questioning. If the right questions are not asked during discovery, then when the salesperson arrives at the finish line, she won't have the information needed to keep the deal energized. Most important, she won't have the tools needed to win the deal at the prices she wants.

I'm going to take you to a place I'm sure you don't want to go: the dentist's chair. You are there for a routine cleaning and exam. After the hygienist performs your teeth cleaning, the dentist enters the room armed with a sharp metal-hooked instrument.

"Lie back and open your mouth wide," the dentist says.

He shines a bright light into your mouth, grabs that sharp metal-hooked instrument, and proceeds to enter your mouth with the device. The dentist places the instrument on the tooth farthest in the back of your mouth and pushes it down to see if it sticks. Methodically, he guides the instrument to each tooth in your mouth, one by one, using the same process.

"Just about done," you think. "Only one tooth left."

Then, it happens. The hook sticks in the final tooth of the examination. "Ugh!"

"Uh-oh," the dentist says as he prepares to conduct a deeper analysis of the tooth. "You may have a cavity. I'm going to need to do some testing to determine the issue with it."

He then turns the entire focus of the exam toward that tooth to determine the *root* cause of the issue and the severity of the cavity. His objective is to determine a comprehensive understanding of the problem and develop an appropriate solution.

The initial exam with the sharp metal-hooked instrument was just a scan. The hook didn't solve any problems. It enabled the dentist to discover where further exploration was needed to develop a comprehensive picture of the issue.

I share this uncomfortable dental story in contrast to the discovery phase of the new client acquisition process. During discovery, salespeople typically ask one type of question. However, in most cases, they should be asking two types.

Horizontal and *Vertical Questions*

Returning to discovery, initial scan questions are what I refer to as *Horizontal Questions*. These questions uncover "the what." They help you identify potential areas of pain or challenge that a DI may be experiencing.

Salespeople typically neglect to ask what I call *Vertical Questions*. These questions uncover "the why." They should be asked when the hook sticks in the tooth. *Vertical Questions* are intended to provide a comprehensive analysis of the pain/challenge the DI is experiencing to determine the proper course of action. When sales managers perceive closing issues, I suggest they ask their salespeople *Vertical Questions* to expose the actual issue.

> *Vertical Questions* are intended to provide a comprehensive analysis of the pain/challenge the DI is experiencing to determine the proper course of action.

For example, a sales manager tells me that their salesperson asked the DI when they wanted a new system implemented. The DI responded, "In August."

The salesperson wrote down "August" in his portfolio and moved on to the next question.

Asking "When would you like to see a new system implemented?" is a *Horizontal Question*. It tells you "the what," but not "the why." *Horizontal Questions* do not provide the salesperson with the tools needed to advance the deal because of the unknown "why" behind it. That's what *Vertical Questions* provide.

The mystery solver in me wants to know so much more than the date the DI wants a new system implemented.

Here are *Vertical Questions* that could have been asked by the salesperson based on the "August" response:

- What is magical about August for an implementation date?
- What are the ramifications if a new system is not implemented by that date?

- How long have you had the current system?
- Why haven't you already changed to a new system?
- What have you tried with the current system to adjust it to meet today's needs?
- What were the results of their attempts to adjust the system to meet today's needs?
- Who selected the current system?
- What was the criteria used to select the current system?
- How does that selection criteria affect selection of the new system?
- What other systems and processes are affected by changing systems?
- Can the other systems and processes affect the timeline for implementation?
- How will you personally be impacted if that implementation date is not met?
- How important is it to you to implement a new system by that date? Why?
- How important is it to the company to implement a new system by that date? Why?
- Is this issue worth solving now? Why?
- What needs to happen for that August implementation date to be achieved?
- Who needs to be involved for that August implementation timeline to be achieved?
- What would keep that implementation date from being achieved?

I'll bet you could add to that list of *Vertical Questions*, but the takeaway is the concept of being insatiable in your quest to fully analyze an opportunity. This list of questions provides a comprehensive analysis of "August," and together the questions answer "the why."

In this case, capturing the desired installation date is merely a data point. By itself, it does not provide what you need to keep your deal energized and win it at the prices you want. Don't just write down the date and move on to your next question. You may think the deal is progressing, but it hasn't moved an inch. More important, you lack the information to keep the deal moving forward, which becomes painfully apparent when expected award dates don't happen.

An Inconvenience or a Problem?

Just about every sales book ever written preaches the importance of salespeople finding pain and challenges that DIs are experiencing during discovery. When salespeople hear about a DI's challenges, they start licking their chops because they believe the door has opened to their solution. Unfortunately, many of them become disappointed when their deals never advance past the initial conversation.

What's the reason for these stalled deals? Salespeople haven't used *Vertical Questions* to determine if the pain they have uncovered is an "inconvenience" or a "problem" for the DI. Those two words are not synonymous.

An inconvenience is merely an annoyance. It's bothersome. In our everyday lives, we all encounter these hassles. However, we don't do anything about them. We live with them until an issue elevates to the level of a problem. This is important to remember. Just because the issue causes a headache doesn't mean DIs will take action to address it. Actually, few will do anything about inconveniences.

DIs take action when they face a problem. When this happens, they recognize that immediate action needs to be taken to address it. The search for solutions has begun. DIs will invest time, resources, and dollars to solve a problem, but not necessarily an inconvenience. People solve problems with solutions.

Here's where many salespeople get stuck. They don't ask *Vertical Questions* to determine if the shared challenge is something the DI can either live with or is ready to address. If you don't definitively know the answer to that question, ask *Vertical Questions* (like the ones shared on the prior pages) to understand their perspective.

Sometimes, salespeople see issues as problems when their DIs only perceive them as inconveniences. This is an important opportunity salespeople have to create energy in their deals. Through *Horizontal* and *Vertical Questions*, salespeople can help DIs view the issue as a problem, create a sense of urgency to address the problem, and motivate them to take action on it.

Also, the DI you are speaking with may feel an issue is a problem, but their colleagues and superiors don't perceive it that way. How do you know if the other DIs feel the same way? Ask! Using *Vertical Questions*, ask the DI if others in the organization feel the same way they do about the issue. For example, "Do your colleagues view this as an inconvenience or a problem?" That question will be met by a brief silence as they consider how others feel. Then they will share their perspective. If other heavily influential DIs don't also see it as a problem, the deal has a high risk of stalling. If they share the same perspective as your DI, the deal has energy to proceed.

The "Closing" Issue

Both *Horizontal* and *Vertical Questions* are needed to keep energy alive in your deals. *Vertical Questions* provide you with the tools needed when stalls occur.

"We decided to hold off on implementing a new system," the DI says after reviewing your proposal.

The salesperson who only asked *Horizontal Questions* panics because he recognizes he's stuck. All he knows is the month the DI wants to implement a new solution. But answers to *Vertical Questions* would have provided the tools to reenergize the deal.

With that information in hand, the salesperson could have had a conversation with the DI that sounded like this:

"Thank you for sharing with me the decision to hold off on implementing a new system. I'm puzzled by what you shared with me when we met a few weeks ago. You mentioned that implementing a new system was critical to both you and the company because the current system is not reliable, is causing you to overstaff by 20 percent to support it, and is causing operations to miss several key performance metrics. May I ask what changed?"

By asking *Vertical Questions,* the salesperson has an opportunity to resurrect the deal or at least to pivot to a different solution, given the additional information provided by the DI. By not asking *Vertical Questions,* however, the salesperson has no choice but to go into the CRM and mark the deal "dead."

This also leads to a related discovery issue that creates the perception that there is a closing problem. In B2B sales, salespeople often don't uncover the business drivers for the solutions they sell. Business drivers are numeric. They have financial impacts such as revenue increases, cost reductions, and efficiency gains. If there is a business case for what you sell, it is critical to capture the strong business drivers for the deal using *Vertical Questions.* Most DIs are not going to support buying your product, service, or technology simply because it "makes things easier." *Vertical Questions* lead you to uncover the DI's perception of the financial impact your solution can have on their business. Without knowing this information, the path leading to the finish line for your deal is paved with quicksand.

Training Yourself to Ask *Vertical Questions*

Why don't salespeople naturally ask *Vertical Questions*? While I do not have a degree in psychology, I do have a perspective on this topic. I'm a firm believer that it dates back to childhood. Salespeople don't ask enough questions during discovery because of their parents.

If there is a business case for what you sell, it is critical to capture the strong business drivers for the deal using *Vertical Questions*.

Young children ask their parents tons of questions. "Why is the sky blue?" "Why is that so small?" "When are we going to be there?" Parents tolerate a few questions and then firmly slam the door shut. "It just is. No more questions." We've been conditioned not to ask too many questions because people will get annoyed with us, which makes salespeople too timid during discovery.

One of the key ingredients in what I call the Sales Success Recipe, the makeup of a top-performing salesperson, is being naturally inquisitive. This is someone who is insatiable in their quest to solve sales mysteries. This salesperson recognizes that key deal "evidence" is uncovered in discovery.

Because of the "parental issue," *Vertical Questions* do not come naturally for most salespeople, so we need to train our brains to think in this fashion. I have developed a series of exercises to reprogram your mind to think in terms of *Vertical Questions*. These exercises will help you develop the mastery to capture a complete picture during discovery. Then you can craft the right solution while keeping the deal energized.

Provided in the exercises are single pieces of information shared by a DI in response to a *Horizontal Question*. For each one, write down as many *Vertical Questions* as you can in three minutes. For some of these, I've had coaching clients develop over fifty *Vertical Questions* based on just that one nugget of information.

Don't try to complete all of the exercises in one day. This is meant to be training for your mind, so pick one exercise per day (or per week) to complete. Better yet, try these exercises as a group activity with your colleagues. At the end of the three-minute period, compare question lists. If each of you came up with ten questions, I'll bet only half would overlap, meaning each of you can improve on your *Vertical Question* strategy. Here are the responses to *Horizontal Questions*:

THE MYTH OF CLOSING PROBLEMS

- "I want to get in shape."
- "I want red wallpaper."
- "I want cardboard boxes."
- "I want mulch for my garden."
- "I want a mechanical pencil."
- "I want a blue rug."
- "I want a smartphone."
- "I want to get married."
- "I want a laptop computer."
- "I want a suitcase."
- "I want a couch."
- "I want a television."
- "I want a wood door."
- "I want to go on vacation."

Ready to raise the bar and try some more challenging ones? Here are four more responses for *Vertical Questions* brain training:

- "I want to outsource an administrative function."
- "I want to automate our operations processes."
- "I want to reduce error rates in operations."
- "I want to buy a CRM."

When executives perceive closing issues, the Discovery *Sell Different!* strategy reveals the true problem, provides the solution, and keeps deals energized.

DISCOVERY *SELL DIFFERENT!* CONCEPT

Comprehensive discovery is the critical foundation needed to keep deals energized and win them at the prices you want.

CHAPTER 8

DISSECTING THE TOUGHEST
SALES OBJECTION

I f you read my book *Sales Differentiation,* you probably raised your eyebrows as you read the title of this chapter. In that book, I shared my perspective on Deal Obstacles that salespeople encounter along the way to winning a deal. I don't see Deal Obstacles as objections, but rather as concerns Decision Influencers share. When salespeople perceive those as objections, their selling strategy is to fight. They must overcome objections. When they see those as DI concerns, their strategy is to sit on the same side of the desk as the DI (figuratively, not literally) and work together to resolve them.

Rest assured, my perspective on Deal Obstacles has not changed. I still firmly believe that salespeople should seek to resolve concerns, not try to overcome objections. However, most of the selling universe still uses the expression "objections," so I used that terminology as the title for this chapter. But that is not how I suggest you navigate Deal Obstacles.

I'll bet when you read the title, you knew the subject this chapter addresses. Most salespeople say the number one sales challenge they face is price. They present a price to a DI and are told that it is too high.

> Salespeople should seek to resolve concerns, not try to overcome objections.

They are left with two choices: lose the deal or drop the price. As part of my consulting work, I review past sales pipelines and conduct postmortem analyses on lost deals. Commonly, salespeople say they lost a deal because of their "price." The truth is that deals are never lost due to price.

When DIs tell salespeople they selected an alternative option because it was cheaper, most salespeople perceive the reason for the loss was that their price was too high. While that may be what the DI said, it wasn't the actual cause for the lost deal. When DIs raise that issue, it's not a price balk. They are providing salespeople with constructive criticism. They are saying that the value demonstrated is not commensurate with the price presented. Thinking in terms of two sides of a scale, when the price issue arises, the price side of the scale outweighs the methods the salesperson used to differentiate both what they sell and how they sell. They have not demonstrated enough meaningful value to the DI to support the price of the presented solution.

Barking Up the Wrong Tree

In the introduction to this book, I shared that my inspiration for *Sales Differentiation* came from my job as a driver for a dry-cleaning transportation service. One of the takeaway messages from that venture was the importance of determining the right people to pursue when selling. Those people who had a way to transport their laundry to and from the dry cleaner and had the time to do it felt our pricing was "out of whack." Were they wrong? Absolutely not! They were 100 percent right. What we were selling was not a fit for everyone. Only those who lacked the means or time to transport their laundry saw value in the service offered.

Salespeople often make the same mistake Dave did when he first started selling that dry-cleaning transportation service. They waste time chasing deals that have no chance of being won at the prices they want because those buyers will never perceive enough value in the offering.

This is another reason why I don't use the expression "Ideal Client Profile." It sends the wrong message to salespeople and leads to a continuum of pricing issues. The word "Ideal" implies that this is an opportunity the company would love to have, but it is a rarity. On the other hand, "Target Client Profile" clearly tells you the attributes of the accounts to pursue: those who will see value in what you sell. This lays a foundation for your Pricing *Sell Different!* strategy.

Value perception is also about selecting the right point of entry into an account. Before sending a prospecting email or making a prospecting call, think about who would perceive the most value in what you are selling. If what you sell has a major impact on the financials of the company, the best entry point is represented by those DIs with Profit & Loss (P&L) responsibilities. They will see the most value in what you offer.

Total Cost of Ownership and Return on Investment

When my daughter, Jamie, was looking for her first college apartment, she found one building that was an absolute palace. She described it to me cautiously because she "knew" it was financially out of reach.

"The building is amazing," she said. "There is a gym on the first floor, each apartment is fully furnished, and every bedroom and living room has a flat-screen television."

We continued talking and she told me about a second apartment she was considering. The rent for that apartment was $100 per month lower than "the palace" and she was strongly considering signing a lease there. She went on to tell me that, for this apartment, we would need to buy bedroom and living room furniture as well as a television. Plus, she wanted to work out and would need a gym membership.

As much as she really wanted the more expensive apartment, she was resigned to accept the cheaper one. I asked her, "Why do you think this apartment is cheaper?"

She looked at me puzzled and said, "The rent is $100 lower."

"That is true, but what about the furniture, the television, and the gym membership we would need to buy if you rent the other apartment?" I responded.

We then made a list of costs for each apartment. Much to her surprise, the higher-rent apartment was the better deal. After giving me a big hug, she immediately signed the lease with a huge smile on her face. She had just learned about a very important sales concept called "Total Cost of Ownership" (TCO).

I should have received a commission for this sale. After all, I did the work the higher-price salesperson should have done. He would have unnecessarily lost a deal over my daughter's perception of higher price. Salespeople cannot rely on DIs, or fathers, to analyze their pricing to determine if it is a good deal or not. That responsibility rests firmly on salespeople.

One of the mistakes commonly made when selling something that has a strong TCO or Return on Investment (ROI) is failure to present a financial model to support it. Salespeople make claims of "huge savings" and "strong TCO and ROI," but they don't make the financial impact tangible for DIs. To help DIs perceive meaningful value in your solution, develop models that allow them to enter their data and see the calculated savings for themselves. Don't rely on telling them about the financial impact in generalities. That lacks "oomph." It doesn't sound believable. Help them see the impact for themselves.

Effectively demonstrating ROI is one of the best ways to neutralize price concerns. If your solution costs a nickel more than the alternative, but yours can provide twice the TCO/ROI, you should win those deals at the prices you want all day long. The key is to connect *logic* (financial) with their *emotions* (how they feel about the financial impact) during discovery as mentioned in the last chapter to win the deal at the prices you want.

Sometimes data to calculate the impact is not available or the DI doesn't want to share it with you. When you design your TCO/ROI models, have placeholder numbers or calculations based on assumptions, so you can calculate TCO/ROI even if the DI doesn't have precise data to enter.

A great example of the need for a TCO/ROI model occurs when selling computer printers. Let's say the printer that you are selling is priced higher than the competitor's. However, your ink cartridges, which is where printer manufacturers really make money, last longer than the competitor's. Over time, your solution is less expensive than theirs. But don't expect your DI to figure that out. You will need a TCO/ROI model that demonstrates cost per page printed, which, in this case, would be in your favor, and eliminate the price concern.

When you are selecting potential accounts and determining proper entry points, your strategy should be to pursue only those who will perceive value in what you offer. This helps you avoid wasting critical selling time with those who will never buy what you sell at the prices you want.

Does Price Really Matter?

Salespeople are hypersensitive about the subject of price. Rarely do they feel their price is too low for the marketplace, but rather too high. Salespeople waste an abundance of time and energy on this. Yes, what you sell has to be priced commensurate with the value provided, but the responsibility to demonstrate that value to DIs falls on the shoulders of salespeople.

Before that burden can be placed on salespeople's shoulders, the executive team has responsibilities to fulfill. Too many companies fail to teach salespeople how to demonstrate meaningful value to DIs. In some cases, the executives themselves cannot clearly articulate the strategy to demonstrate meaningful value in what their salespeople are selling. Before salespeople can be taught, the company needs to create the value demonstration strategy.

Executives may leave value demonstration up to the salespeople, which is a surefire recipe for disaster. Some salespeople will eventually figure it out, but the majority won't. To be clear, it is the executive team's responsibility to develop their Pricing *Sell Different!* strategy to demonstrate meaningful value. Once that is defined, they need to teach their salespeople how to execute the strategy. Then, and only then, it becomes the salespeople's responsibility to follow that strategy to win more deals at the prices they want.

Without that teaching in place, you'll either continually drop prices to win deals or have a revolving door of salespeople who don't perform at the desired levels.

While salespeople are oversensitive about the effect of price, perhaps they are placing too much emphasis on it. If price is the be-all, end-all decision factor, then we all would:

- Wear the cheapest clothes.
- Live in the cheapest houses.

- Eat the cheapest food.
- Use the cheapest toilet paper.

- Have the cheapest phones.
- Sit in the worst seats at the ballgame.

- Drive the cheapest cars.
- Shave with a single-blade razor.

Remember, many people have bought from your company. I'll bet it wasn't because of low price. It was the meaningful value that salespeople demonstrated during the new client acquisition process.

If you don't know the reasons why DIs bought from you, add that action item to your "to-do" list. Don't guess the answers. You need factual information. Recently, I was competing against a few of the largest sales training companies in the world as well as some sole practitioners for a deal. I won the deal (yes, at the prices I wanted). I thought I knew why they selected my firm, but I asked during the kickoff call. If I relied on my assumptions, I would have been dead wrong. You have to ask your clients why they selected you, so you can learn from that experience and use it to win more deals at the prices you want.

Losing a deal shouldn't be entirely bad news. Sure, we would all love to win every deal, but that's not a realistic expectation in any selling environment. No salespeople are expected to win 100 percent of their deals. A lost deal should be a learning experience for you and your company. I encourage sales managers to reach out to DIs when deals are lost and request a brief phone conversation. The intent is not to change the DI's mind. It's to find out where the company went wrong and find out the reason for the loss. If they say it was due to price, it means that the salesperson failed to demonstrate enough meaningful value to support the presented price.

Does price matter? Absolutely! No one, including you and me, is willing to pay one penny more than we need to. If we do not perceive meaningful value, price will always be the determining factor. The burden falls on salespeople to demonstrate meaningful value in support of their pricing.

The Flinch Test

After a lengthy new client acquisition process, the time has come to submit a proposal including pricing. Countless hours are spent formulating a glorious proposal that details your comprehensive solution. Proud of your accomplishment, you present the proposal to your DI. Skipping the "About Your Company" and "Your Solution" sections, she flips right to the pricing page and says, "Oh my gosh, I didn't think it would be this expensive!"

What happens next determines whether or not you will win the deal at the prices you want. There is a trade secret in the purchasing world. I call it "The Flinch Test." This is the test procurement agents and other professional buyers give to salespeople when they present pricing.

"Wow! You are 25 percent higher than your competitor." These buying pros are trained to react with surprise, in an effort to see if the salesperson is confident in the price they have put forward. It is nothing more than a negotiation tactic. Sometimes they overstate the price difference such that you can perform some quick math and see that their claim about your competitor is bogus.

I recall a time when a procurement agent claimed we were 50 percent higher than the competition. I reviewed the numbers and saw that if this were true, then the competitor was losing 18 percent based on fixed costs that we both had. It was highly unlikely that the competitor was selling this kind of a deal. When I asked the procurement agent about that 50 percent figure, he *flinched.* Ultimately, we won the deal at the prices we wanted.

Salespeople are evaluated based on sales metrics. Procurement agents are measured against purchasing metrics. Performance against those metrics can affect their salaries and bonuses. They have an obligation to ask you for a lower price as they are acting in the best interests of their employer. That doesn't mean you need to give it to them, but they have to ask, so be prepared.

The key to passing "The Flinch Test" is to respond with confidence in your price. If you don't believe you are providing a fair price for the solution, then why are you presenting it? One would hope that you have integrity, so why present something you don't believe in?

Some sales responses that guarantee you will fail "The Flinch Test" include:

- "What price were you looking for?"
- "I'll ask my manager if we can do better."
- "How about if I take 10 percent off?"

These are failed responses because they create trust issues with the DI. Were you trying to "rip them off" with the price you presented? One of two things is true. Either you were trying to take advantage of them, or you believe you provided a fair price. What other option is there?

Some salespeople say that they were expecting a negotiation. That's a fair point; however, it is a terrible negotiation strategy to give the appearance that you will drop your price the moment someone balks. That approach gives the impression that you sought to gouge them. Good luck having a healthy relationship with a client after that.

Most negotiations end at the middle ground. They wanted five; you wanted ten and settled at seven point five. That seems logical. However, if you immediately lower your price, the middle ground becomes lower. In the same scenario, if you dropped to eight right off the bat, the middle becomes six point five. As I mentioned, you have to manage the negotiation such that the middle is not lower than the level at which you want to win the deal.

Successful salespeople have a planned, or dare I say "canned," response for "The Flinch Test." They don't expect a DI to respond with excitement about the proposed price. They anticipate shock and have methods to handle it. Here are their secrets:

- **Set expectations up front.** Early in the process, they set the expectation that they are not the low-price provider. "To be clear, our company is rarely the low bid. Does that mean that we won't be working together on this project?" If they say no, you are set for the later phases of the process. If they say yes, you can ask about the impact ROI and TCO have on their decision-making. If that doesn't matter to them either, you know not to invest an excessive amount of time on an account that you won't win at the prices you want. If you are going to lose, lose early.
- **Don't flinch!** They say, "I'm not surprised by your reaction. I hear that a lot. As I mentioned at the outset, we are rarely the

low bidder. Should we walk through the proposal again to make sure you are comparing apples to apples?" This is the opportunity to remind them of your differentiators and the meaningful value your solution provides.

- **Seek to understand.** They ask, "When you say that you are shocked by the price, which part is surprising?" You need to know what part of the pricing they feel is out of line, so you can appropriately address it.

- **Gain clarity on the DI's perspective.** They inquire, "When you say our pricing is high, what is that relative to?" Don't ever guess. Ask! They may be comparing it to something you had not considered. It could be to their budget, to their current solution, to another bidder, or to doing it themselves. To respond effectively, you have to know the basis of the comparison.

- **Reinforce the position.** They ask, "Since we are rarely the low-price provider, what do you think our one thousand clients see in us, versus the competition, that leads them to pay a little more for our solution?" This question helps the DI reconsider their perspective on the pricing for your solution.

If you are going to give something, you need to get something. If you are willing to make a price concession, what is the DI willing to offer you in return that justifies it? The "get something" should be something of value to you and your company, such as:

- Increasing order size (volume).
- Accelerating payment for the order.
- Extending length of the purchasing agreement.
- Reducing the scope/requirements of the deal.
- Taking delivery earlier/later than you proposed.
- Facilitating introductions to senior executives in other business units or to colleagues in other companies.

- Participating in an interview with your marketing department to develop a case study.
- Serving as a reference when needed.

I'm often asked by executives and salespeople to name the best sales training program I have ever participated in. Expecting me to name one of the world's top sales training firms, they are always surprised by my answer.

Many years ago, I had the opportunity to participate in procurement agent training. It was the best training ever! Think of it as sales training for buyers. I felt like a spy because I was learning the methods professional buyers were being taught to use when procuring products and services.

During a break, I had an interesting conversation with the instructor about the price issue. Here's what he told me:

> "For twenty-five years, salespeople have asked me for coaching on the price of their proposal as I was the procurement head for my company. I told each one of them the same thing. 'Give us the best price that you feel good about giving us and, either way, you win.' I always got a puzzled expression from that response."
>
> He went on to explain, "If we award the business to you at that price, you're happy. If we award the business to someone else at a lower price, you are happy as well because you wouldn't have been happy to support our account at that price point."

To share a little secret, I use "The Flinch Test" all the time when I make purchases. It's amazing how quickly salespeople drop their prices. I bet I've saved my family 20 percent, across the board, for all of our spending just by having a reaction when a price is presented to me. It's no wonder that professional buyers use this technique. How many commission dollars are lost just because salespeople flinched? How many commission dollars have you lost because you flinched?

How many commission dollars have you lost because you flinched?

Understanding the Why

Many salespeople mistakenly think they understand the DI's concern when the price issue is raised. A fatal flaw for your deal, indeed! The truth is that the cause for this concern isn't initially known. A myriad of possibilities could be causing this concern.

- Is it a question of how much use they will get from the product?
- Is it whether or not they can afford it?
- Is it that they saw a similar product at a cheaper price?

There are others, but you get the point. Bottom line: without knowing what is causing the price concern, you can't possibly help the DI work through it. To share a personal example, I live in Minnesota where owning a boat is commonplace. Per capita, no state has more boat owners than Minnesota. To me, however, boat ownership is expensive. It isn't the price of the boat, or the cost of maintenance, or even the price of the slip. It is the fact that the boating season is so short here that I don't feel I would get enough usage out of it to justify the financial investment.

On the other hand, I bought battery-operated cars for my three kids when they were young. Each vehicle had a three-hundred-dollar price tag on it. Expensive to some, but cheap to me. Why? Because my kids used them for years. From my perspective, it was worth every penny. If I get significant utility out of something, I can justify the price in my mind.

At the other end of the spectrum, like most parents, I have bought tons of toys in the twenty-dollar price range that have been used once, maybe twice. After that, they are never touched again. To me, that is expensive.

Some other price concerns center on whether or not they can financially afford the proposed solution. Some salespeople focus on budget to determine whether or not their solution will fit within it. Why limit yourself to budget? Better yet, what if there is no budget for what you sell?

I'm a sales management strategist. No company ever has a budget for me. However, if you work with DIs at a high enough level in the organization and demonstrate enough meaningful value, pricing becomes a non-issue. From my experience, mid-level managers are constrained by budgets. High-level executives find dollars when they find a solution that provides meaningful value. Invest your time on those who can innovate budgets, not those constrained by them.

> Invest your time on those who can innovate budgets, not those constrained by them.

Sometimes the pricing issue comes up because the DI has seen the same product, or a similar one, at a lower price. When I worked in the employment background screening industry, DIs would compare a $9.95 database search with a comprehensive criminal courthouse search. The comparison of the two was an apples and oranges scenario in terms of the price and the solution itself. The strong salespeople were able to explain the difference in a way that led DIs to see that they needed the comprehensive search.

The $9.95 search was actually more expensive than the comprehensive search because so few convictions were identified from it. Those clients were paying for a service that yielded little or no benefit to their hiring process.

Buyers don't have an issue with price. Their issue is a lack of meaningful value commensurate with the price you presented. What is absolutely critical is that you must believe in that value. If you don't wholeheartedly believe what you're selling is worth its price tag, find another job! If you don't believe in your price, I guarantee you that no one else will either.

PRICING *SELL DIFFERENT!* CONCEPT

Pursue only those accounts and Decision Influencers who will perceive meaningful value in what you sell and can create budgets rather than be constrained by them.

CHAPTER 9

THE ULTIMATE DEAL KILLER

A very Brandon is eagerly waiting in the lobby for his meeting with Regina Jacobs of ABC Industries. The other day, Avery had a great initial phone conversation with her, resulting in the scheduling of today's discovery meeting. Avery's fingers are crossed because he is not on track to achieve his annual revenue target. He really needs this deal to come together.

Regina enters the lobby with a smile on her face and shakes Avery's hand. She escorts him back to her office and invites him to sit down in a chair across from her desk.

After they exchange pleasantries, Avery begins, "Regina, what was it I said on the phone that led you to take a meeting with me?"

"Where do I begin?" Regina responds in frustration. "We are having serious problems with our current supplier. What we order and what we receive are two completely different things. And what we do receive from them arrives later than the committed date. When we talk with our account manager about these issues, he is not responsive and has not solved the problems. My team is at wits' end with this supplier. When you contacted me, I felt the time had come for us to investigate our options."

Hearing her concerns, Avery tries not to salivate. His company shines when it comes to order accuracy and delivery timeliness. He prides himself on being both a responsive and a proactive account manager. Clients frequently email raves to his manager about the service he provides.

Constraining his excitement, Avery begins to share how his company handles accounts similar to hers. He also talks about the way he personally manages his clients.

Regina leans back in her chair and says, "You are almost too good to be true. You have made my day! If we were to change suppliers to you, how quickly could we get started?"

Avery feels like he has won the lottery. After about an hour with Regina, he heads back to his car. Rather than wait until he returns to the office, he calls his sales manager from Regina's parking lot to share the great news.

"I just had an amazing discovery meeting with Regina Jacobs of ABC Industries. She has numerous challenging issues with her current supplier and those issues are our strengths. She asked how quickly we could transition her account to us. This is a done deal!"

Over the next few weeks, Avery attempts to contact Regina to continue their conversation and advance the process. Yet, she doesn't respond to his emails or voicemails. This is surprising to Avery, given the tone of their initial meeting.

Friday morning, Avery receives an email from Regina:

Avery,

I'm sorry for being slow to respond. I appreciate you meeting with me. After much thought, we have decided not to make a change now.

Regards,
Regina

Avery's heart sinks. This deal was going to make his year and now it is dead. He doesn't know where he went wrong, and now he dreads having to tell his sales manager this awful news.

What was Avery's mistake?

A Decision Influencer's Paralyzing Fear

There is a potential deal killer in every sale. It doesn't matter if you are a business-to-business, business-to-consumer, or business-to-government salesperson. This risk exists in every deal. Some Decision Influencers will share this concern with you. Others, like Regina, are silent about it, but their actions communicate the deal-killing concern: *fear of change.*

DIs have a moment of pause any time they consider making a change in process or provider. Their minds race as they consider this situation:

> **"While I'm not happy with my current provider, things can always be worse. If I make the decision to change, and the situation worsens, my career with this company could be in jeopardy."**

This fear is so strong, it causes buyer paralysis. Even though they know their current situation is awful, they are afraid to take the steps necessary to improve it. There's an old proverb: *Better the devil you know than the devil you don't.* This proverb gives DIs pause.

There's also an old sales joke related to this issue. A man is on his deathbed and just before he passes away, the devil comes to see him.

The devil says, "You have probably heard some terrible things about Hell, but they are not true. Take a little trip with me and see for yourself."

The man agrees and visits Hell with the devil. The devil was right. The weather was beautiful, the food was delicious.

The man says to the devil, "This place is amazing. When I die, I'm coming here."

The next day, the man passes away and goes to Hell. Yet, it's nothing like what he had experienced the day prior. The weather was awful. The food was terrible. Frustrated, he tracks down the devil to ask what happened.

> The sales profession has taken a black eye because of weak salespeople who lie and overset expectations with DIs.

"I don't understand," he says to the devil. "Yesterday, the weather was perfect and the food was amazing. Today, both are horrible. What happened?"

The devil grins and says, "Yesterday, you were a prospect."

This joke illustrates a buyer's *fear of change*. The sales profession has taken a black eye because of weak salespeople who lie and overset expectations with DIs. Most DIs fear being duped by slick salespeople. While what they are hearing is compelling, it stops them from inking the deal because they understand that, like the man on his deathbed, they aren't yet a client, but a prospect.

In 2019, Gartner conducted a study regarding the number of people involved in corporate purchase decision-making. They found that an average of 6.8 people are involved in those decisions. Just two years earlier, in another Gartner study, only 5.4 people were involved in the decision-making process. While Gartner does not say or infer this, I believe that one of the primary reasons for the increase in the number of people involved in the decision-making process is the *fear of change*. No one wants to be the one left "holding the bag" if something goes wrong. The more people involved in decision-making, the more the blame can be spread around, along with the risk.

There is a way for you to defeat the *fear of change* and give DIs confidence in your company's ability to perform as expected. In other words, this is an opportunity for a Client Onboarding *Sell Different!* strategy.

Defining Client Onboarding

The key to resolving a DI's *fear of change* is to define the implementation process with your company. You may call it "implementation," "transition," or "client onboarding." However you refer to it, this is the phase that begins when the DI says, "Yes! We want to switch to you," and ends when they are fully functional with your company. This is the process whereby a client moves from their current circumstance to working with your company. It gives DIs confidence that there is a structured plan in place to guide the transition. It resolves *fear-of-change* concerns regarding risk, time, and pain. As I'll explain later in the chapter, this is a process to be productized for salespeople.

Whoops! I used the word "process," implying that all companies have this type of a plan in place. Some companies do, but unfortunately many do not. Of the companies that have a process for this transition, few have defined client onboarding in a way that can be described to DIs. Yet, unless you just opened for business, your company has a method for transitioning clients to begin buying or receiving what you sell.

If your company has not documented its client onboarding process, that is what needs to happen first. Think of client onboarding as a project. You'll need a project plan for onboarding new clients. While there will be nuances from client to client, you should be able to capture the overarching framework.

Here is my thirteen-step process to develop your Client Onboarding *Sell Different!* strategy:

STEP 1: EXPECTATIONS

Imagine a new client has been fully onboarded with your company. What do you expect them to *KNOW*, be able to *DO*, and be able to *USE*?

KNOW refers to information like the products and services available to them and how to contact your customer service department.

DO is an action such as placing an order or scheduling service.

USE refers to systems such as your website or order management system.

Your *KNOW-DO-USE* list will drive the rest of the process.

STEP 2: PROCESS

Based on the identified client expectations in Step 1, define the client onboarding process. To achieve each of the client onboarding expectations, make a list of what needs to happen, by whom, and when. Identify areas on the list that can be personalized for the new client. The process should be firm, but flexible enough to be tailored to each client. For example, if your company has a client portal, someone at the client's company will need access and maybe a little help with navigation before they place their first order.

STEP 3: PLANNING

To accelerate the process and to make it painless for new clients, make a list of everything the client needs to prepare ahead of the transition. Examples include assembling a list of website users, organizing documentation, and preparing historical data you will need from them.

STEP 4: COLLABORATION

Determine which departments and individuals on your team will be involved in client onboarding and the role each person will play. One person should serve as the primary communicator, guiding the client through the onboarding process. Having a single point of contact helps to ensure healthy communication between the two organizations.

STEP 5: SETUP

Identify the behind-the-scenes account setup requirements that are necessary for your back-office systems. These considerations will allow future clients to begin working with you. Examples of these requirements include contact information, business rules for the account, and ordering rules.

STEP 6: ORIGINATION

New clients come to you from a variety of circumstances. Perform an assessment to identify each one's starting point. Some may be changing providers; others outsourcing for the first time. The process needs to accommodate a variety of client starting points, which is why I mentioned that it should be both firm and flexible.

STEP 7: COMMUNICATION

Communication during onboarding is critical both internally and externally with the client. Determine what the communication strategy will be to ensure the project stays on track. A best practice is to create a project plan both internally and for the client. And be sure to provide regular project updates.

STEP 8: TRAINING

Determine the training that is required for different levels of users within the client company and how that training will be provided. If you have different types of users and training formats (such as in person, online, or app), identify which approach is appropriate for each one.

STEP 9: DURATION

Identify the expected duration of client onboarding from contract signing to the client being fully transitioned into your company. It does not need to be an exact number of days or weeks. Having a range is perfectly acceptable. However, identify the tasks that cause either the acceleration or delay of the process. For example, if the client does not provide the requisite information by certain due dates, the transition duration may become prolonged.

STEP 10: TIMELINE

Plot the timeline, showing milestones in a chart for the client's benefit. Show actions that accelerate and lengthen the client onboarding process. An educated client is a happy client. If they know how to help themselves, the transition process runs much smoother.

STEP 11: TRANSITION

Determine the role that the salesperson should play during client onboarding. In some companies, there is a formal handoff whereby the salesperson transitions the account information to a client onboarding team and exits the process. In other companies, the salesperson stays involved from beginning to end. Clarity about role responsibilities helps to avoid internal frustration and client confusion.

In addition, identify the information the salesperson needs to acquire from the client to initiate the client onboarding process. Some companies have a form to capture all the required information, others have a back-office system for this, while others handle it more informally. The key is for salespeople to have clarity regarding what is expected of them to initiate client onboarding and during the transition process.

STEP 12: KICKOFF

Successful client onboarding projects start with a two-part "kickoff program." First is an internal meeting for representatives from those departments affected by the new client joining the company. Second is a launch meeting with the new client to review the process, phases, timelines, and dependencies. Another topic of discussion with the new client is their definition of success, so you know how you will be evaluated during the transition process. If you know how and what they are tracking, you can focus the client onboarding team on those measures.

STEP 13: FEEDBACK

At the end of the client onboarding process, conduct a survey of the transition experience among the various users and stakeholders to solicit their input. Most important, take action on their feedback. Negative feedback requires a phone call to the client to investigate and resolve issues to solidify the client relationship.

Solicit feedback from your internal team to improve the onboarding experience for the next client. Every client onboarding process is an opportunity for your company to learn and improve. Take advantage of it!

The output from this thirteen-step client onboarding process is beneficial in both B2B and B2C selling environments.

The Client Onboarding Product

Earlier I referenced "productizing" the client onboarding process. Think of your client onboarding methodology as something that is "sold" during the buying process. Give it a branded name to increase its credibility. Salespeople shouldn't wait for a client to ask about the process or casually mention it during the course of conversation. It's a major discussion point for resolving a DI's *fear of change*.

What makes client onboarding productization so important? When a DI is experiencing *fear of change* (and they all do), being able to demonstrate your methodology to transition them to your company is the key to neutralizing that fear. It showcases your expertise and gives DIs confidence that they will receive the benefits you shared with minimal risk during the transition.

Productizing client onboarding means taking the thirteen steps and turning the output from the process into a client-facing document. This document should summarize each phase of the onboarding process along with the timeline. Some common phases include: "Project Launch," "Internal Setup," "Installation," "Delivery," "User Training," "Account Live," and "Feedback."

Can't the salesperson just verbally describe the process? Yes, but it won't be effective. Numerous studies have revealed that 65 percent of the population are visual learners. Most people need to see to understand. If you merely talk about your client onboarding approach, you'll miss the mark two-thirds of the time and risk the *fear of change* killing your deal.

Ideally, your client onboarding product is captured on a single page and is easy for a client to read. The document should resemble both a project plan and a marketing tool because that's exactly what it is. Make it informative and colorful. It should include your logo and company contact information as well.

When should the subject of client onboarding be introduced by the salesperson? Once you are receiving positive buying signs from your DI, say:

> **"Our clients appreciate our onboarding methodology. It carefully guides them through the transition process. Would it be helpful to walk through it?"**

Never just leave the document in a folder and ask them to read it on their own. And never email it to them and ask them to review it. Hopefully, you would never do that with the products you sell. Since client onboarding is now a product of yours as well, handle this product the way you would any other. Walk your DI through the phases of the process and ask for their questions as you share it.

To take advantage of Client Onboarding *Sell Different!* strategy to outsmart, outmaneuver, and outsell the competition, you need to do something the competition does not, and that your DIs will find meaningful. Help them gain confidence in you and your company through productizing the client onboarding experience. This gives them the trust they need to take advantage of the wonderful benefits your company offers. Companies that don't have well-defined client onboarding programs give the appearance of being small and unprofessional, which allows the *fear of change* to win the day.

The Reverse Timeline Approach

This strategy provides the tools for you to motivate your DIs into action using a Reverse Timeline approach. Once your DIs provide you with a date they want to be up and running, share the steps necessary to meet that deadline.

DIs might not recognize everything that needs to be done for their goal date to become a reality.

DIs might not recognize everything that needs to be done for their goal date to become a reality. Given that you now have a Client Onboarding *Sell Different!* strategy, you can help them develop a plan. But be careful: DIs may suffer from "Sideview Mirror Syndrome" where objects are closer than they may appear. Do they know all the tasks that need to be completed in short order? Consider a dialogue like this:

You: When would you like this solution to be up and running?

DI: February 1.

You: Why did you select February 1? (One of multiple *Vertical Questions* to be asked to anchor in the date.)

DI: This allows us to start the program on the same day as the beginning of our fiscal year, which makes it easier for Accounting to manage.

You: Would it be helpful to walk through the steps we need to undergo for February 1 to happen?

DI: That would be very helpful.

You: Once you and your team determine that we are the right solution for your program, our next step is to finalize the agreement with your legal department. How long do you think that will take?

DI: About four weeks.

You: Since today is November 1 and we need to give Legal four weeks to finalize the agreement, that takes us to December 1. The next step would be to have a kickoff call with our respective teams. That means we are looking at the week of December 1 for this step.

DI: That makes sense to me.

You: Normally, it takes about four weeks for the teams to exchange information and have systems properly set up. This takes us to January 8, given the holidays and vacations.

DI: Right . . .

You: The next step is to train your team on the use of the system and that normally takes two weeks to complete. That takes us to the end of January. This means we have about a week for you to determine if we are the right solution for you. After all, neither of us wants to rush the transition and risk errors. Given this timeline, how would you like to proceed?

In addition to walking them through the timeline, offer to send it in an email in case they need to share it with others. This dialogue helps your DIs understand the steps and timing associated with the transition. It also helps them recognize that the decision timeline is shorter than they may think.

Had Avery's company productized client onboarding and guided Regina through the process and timeline, he could have helped her resolve her *fear of change*.

CLIENT ONBOARDING *SELL DIFFERENT!* CONCEPT

Client onboarding is the documented bridge program, connecting Decision Influencers' circumstances to your solution, neutralizing their *fear of change*.

CHAPTER 10

PILOTS, TRIALS, AND TRUST (OR LACK THEREOF)

I n chapter 9, I introduced the Client Onboarding *Sell Different!* strategy to neutralize a Decision Influencer's *fear of change.* Yet, there is a related sales peril of which we also need to be mindful.

After methodically following the process, you present your productized client onboarding program and proposed solution to the DI. She responds by saying, "This looks great. Here's what we want to do next. We want to try your solution for free for thirty days. If that goes well, we will talk about plans to go forward."

Is it time for the "happy dance," or are you seeing warning lights flashing before your eyes? On the one hand, you have taken another step toward winning the deal at the prices you want. On the other hand, you need an effective strategy for that to happen.

Trust

Why do DIs ask to conduct pilot programs before making a full commitment to purchase? Previously, I described a DI's *fear of change* and how productizing client onboarding addresses that concern. There is another time when fear rears its ugly head: when a DI requests a pilot or trial program. DIs look at those programs as ways to minimize their risk by "dipping their toe in the water" before jumping in with both feet. Some DIs think of pilots as establishing "proof of concept" for the proposed solution.

Something related to *fear of change* is at play here, which is *trust*. Requests for pilot programs may reveal their trust concerns. If trust were not an issue, the contract would be signed, client onboarding would be underway, and a check would be in your hands. We can also thank weak salespeople for creating trust issues as they have historically overpromised and underdelivered when selling their solutions.

The trust issue might not reside with you and your way of selling. The DI might not trust her own people to use your solution. "If my people don't use your system the way you described it, we will not receive the Return on Investment you described."

DIs ask to conduct pilot programs for a variety of reasons. Knowing those reasons is a must before agreeing to it. But don't guess the reasons; never assume you know why they want a pilot program. Instead, ask your DI to share their reasons.

One common reason (rarely shared by a DI) is personal risk. If the solution you proposed fails for whatever reason, that DI's career with the company could be at risk. Few share that concern with you, but you should know that it is always in the back of their minds when making a decision. Be sensitive to that point.

Imagine a company is about to select an applicant tracking system to manage their recruiting process. After a tremendous amount of due diligence, the team feels like they have found the right technology solution. But there is a hesitation as they ponder the possibilities of things that could go wrong. What if the technology fails? What if the recruiters won't use the system as it is intended? Will the entire hiring process come to a screeching halt? Who will take the hit if that happens? The ability to "try before buy" provides a sense of security for your DI.

The bottom line is that salespeople must know the reason for the trial before agreeing to conduct it.

When you know a DI's reasons, you have the option to decide whether or not to consent to a pilot program. There is no law that requires you to agree to a DI's request for a pilot program. Some salespeople forget that point. They believe if the DI wants a pilot, then it must happen. I don't subscribe to that philosophy. You have the option to decline it, and should decline, if the reasons for the pilot request or the approach she wants to take do not help you advance the deal.

> The only reason to agree to take on a pilot program or suggest having one is to move the deal forward.

There also may be times you introduce the concept of a pilot program as a strategy to resolve DI skepticism of the proposed solution. It can be an effective way to introduce your solution into an organization and potentially displace a competitor. Again, the only reason to agree to take on a pilot program or suggest having one is to move the deal forward.

Why Thirty Days?

In the example at the beginning of this chapter, the DI asked for a thirty-day trial. But why? What is magical about a month? Why not six days or twenty-eight days? You will need to know the answer to that before agreeing to a trial program. What will the DI measure? What data will they capture? How will they evaluate the success of the program? Those three points affect the duration of the pilot program. A month may be too short to measure what they want to measure; or it could be too long.

It is also important to keep in mind you have a level of expertise to devise your solution that your DIs do not possess. If you are going to conduct a pilot, you should be the one recommending the appropriate duration, given what the DIs want to evaluate. Don't take their requested duration as "law," but rather counsel them to select the right duration based on what they want to assess. Program duration is a collaborative conversation, not a DI demand.

"Free!"

In the request for the pilot program, the DI asked for the pilot to be provided free of charge. How do they get to decide that your solution should be given to them for nothing? We would all love something for nothing, but rarely get it. Of course, a DI's typical comeback when challenged on this is to tell you that your competitor has agreed to conduct the pilot for free. It reminds me of the times when my friend Brian was allowed to do something that I wasn't. I would tell my mother that Brian was permitted to do it as a way to get her approval. She would simply say, "If Brian jumped off the Brooklyn Bridge, would you want to do that too?"

Buyers don't get to demand your solution be provided for free. That is a decision for you to make. Think of the pilot as an investment in the relationship. You get to decide what investment you are willing to make in the deal to increase the likelihood of winning it. Coming back to their point about your competitor, if you are not inclined to offer the pilot for free, ask the DI, "Why would they give their product away for free? Doesn't it have meaningful value?"

A creative hybrid solution to that request is to offer to refund their money if the pilot fails. That way, you both have "skin in the game" and will work together to ensure the pilot is a success.

The Non-Commitment Commitment

The *piece de resistance* in the DI's response is what I call the "non-commitment commitment." "If that goes well, we will talk about plans to go forward." After the pilot program, there will be other hurdles for you to jump through to win the deal at the prices you want.

Let's couple two aspects together. They want a free pilot and they're unwilling to make a commitment based on its success. There are times when it makes sense to provide a free trial for a period of time to demonstrate proof of concept. However, agreeing to the pilot only makes sense if there is a firm commitment to award you the deal if the program is successful.

Ah, but how does one define "successful"? Understanding your DI's definition of success and how they will measure it are critical decision points for you to understand when deciding whether or not to agree to the pilot program. Without having that information, you and your team won't know what the DI's target objectives are. Plus, if their expectations for the pilot are unrealistic, it is important to reset them. If not, then the pilot will fail and you will never be awarded the full deal.

Keys to Success

All of that said, let's say you have decided pilot programs are a critical part of your new client acquisition process as they help you advance deals to the finish line. Here are the twelve steps of my Pilot Program *Sell Different!* strategy.

1. Determine if the DI is conducting this pilot exclusively with you or if she is also conducting a parallel pilot with your competitors. If she is working with your competitors, you have to decide if conducting the pilot program helps or hurts your deal. With other providers still in the mix, determine if conducting a pilot program *now* helps you advance the deal.

2. Fully understand the DI's purpose and intent of the pilot. What does the client hope to accomplish? What do they intend to assess? The pilot goals should be crystal clear to you.

3. Given what the DI wants to accomplish, identify the metrics to be used to gauge success and how that data will be captured. Metrics are specific data points. Be wary of situations in which pilot participant opinions are the sole

measures of success. Instead, your goal should be to have objective data used to assess pilot performance.

4. Set the appropriate length of the pilot program based on how the DI is going to measure success. You should be the driver in determining appropriate pilot program duration as you have a greater expertise in your solution than the DI.

5. Structure the pilot program in such a way that allows you and your company to shine. This includes helping the DI select the right participants.

6. Use your client onboarding program to facilitate the pilot program. This ensures the implementation is flawless and creates a great first impression with the DI and her colleagues.

7. If the pilot program includes use of a product or technology, make sure the users are adequately trained in it. Frustrated users are pilot program killers as well as deal killers.

8. Before the pilot starts, schedule a midpoint and post-trial meeting with your DI (and other key stakeholders) to review pilot performance. Don't wait for the program to be underway to try and set those meetings. Schedule them up front.

9. Before the pilot begins, develop concrete next steps with the client. If the pilot succeeds, what does the client commit to do as a next step? The appropriate answer is a deal award or something close to it. This is especially important if you make any type of price concessions or absorb significant costs to administer the pilot program.

10. During the pilot program, use your Mentor to obtain inside, informal information and feedback that you would not otherwise know. Your Mentor can help you address situations if concerns arise during the pilot.

11. Prepare your company for the pilot program. Make sure all departments and key personnel are aware of it, its success metrics, and its duration. While it is only a pilot program,

your team should treat the DIs the same way they treat fully onboarded clients.

12. As the one who stands to win or lose the deal based on its performance, the salesperson needs to own the pilot's success. Monitor the program metrics, conduct internal meetings, and make sure your DI is delighted every step of the way!

Remember, the sole purpose of conducting pilot programs is to help you advance deals and win them at the prices you want. If pilot programs help you achieve that objective, incorporate this Pilot Program *Sell Different!* strategy into your selling repertoire and continually refine the process.

> Pilot programs are learning experiences for your company.

Pilot programs are learning experiences for your company. After each one, conduct a debriefing meeting with your internal team and identify ways to improve the experience for future pilots. In addition, measure your conversion rates from pilot programs to awarded deals at the prices you want. That data will help validate (or not) the use of pilot programs in your client acquisition process.

Your handling of a pilot program can also differentiate you. The twelve steps of the Pilot Program *Sell Different!* strategy provides you with the tools to create the experience your DIs desire when they want to "try before buy," and lead you to win deals at the prices you want.

PILOT PROGRAM *SELL DIFFERENT!* CONCEPT

Well-structured pilot programs help resolve Decision Influencers' trust issues and give them confidence in your company's ability to perform.

CHAPTER 11

MORE THAN 99.999% OF SALESPEOPLE DON'T DO THIS, BUT THEY SHOULD

B en, an account executive with XYZ, Inc., met with Eric, the Vice President of Operations for ABC Manufacturing. It was the best discovery meeting Ben could ever have imagined. He identified challenges that Eric was having with his current provider. These challenges were painful for Eric, and he was eager to have them resolved. Ben knew that the solutions were things at which his company excelled.

During the meeting, Ben effectively positioned his company's differentiators and Eric "ate them up!" The meeting lasted an hour, but it felt like just a few minutes to Ben. Time flew by! As a result of the meeting, both Ben and Eric had action items to complete. This deal looked good. Ben was confident he would add it to the win column.

As Ben drove back to his office, the meeting replayed in his head like his favorite movie. He vividly remembered every word Eric spoke, every detail that was shared, and Eric's reactions to what his company offered.

The Big Sales Misstep

Ben assumed that Eric remembered their meeting just as vividly as he did. That is a mistake that many salespeople make. It didn't dawn on him that on the day of their meeting Eric had seven other meetings. He also received about two hundred emails and fourteen voicemails. Each one of those messages layered on top of the meeting with Ben, making it a distant memory for Eric.

Many salespeople are egocentric when they reflect on meetings they have conducted with Decision Influencers. While this deal is so important to salespeople, they forget that what they do represents a fraction of a DI's overall responsibilities. Plus, DIs have so much information coming at them that it is difficult for them to remember it all.

It is for these reasons that more than 99.999% of salespeople miss out on a critical *Sell Different!* strategy that will help keep their deal in the forefront of their DIs' minds.

Another Way to Outsmart, Outmaneuver, and Outsell the Competition

The question we need to ask ourselves is how to keep our deal on track. The answer to that question is the Recap Email *Sell Different!* strategy. The core of this strategy is an email sent by the salesperson to the DI that summarizes the meeting and reminds the DI of the key points discussed.

I'm amazed at how few salespeople send Recap Emails after an initial meeting with a DI, not to mention sending one after every meeting. This Recap Email *Sell Different!* strategy is a creative way to differentiate yourself while keeping the energy alive in your deal. The email message should not, in any way, come across as "salesy." What it should do is quickly remind the DI of the meeting content.

> The email message should not, in any way, come across as "salesy."

Another great reason to send Recap Emails is the number of people involved in the typical B2B decision-making process. As referenced earlier, a Gartner study revealed that an average of 6.8 people are involved in the typical B2B decision-making process. Ben met with only one of the DIs during this meeting. That's a vulnerability, but it's also an opportunity. While he only met with one, he can use the Recap Email to engage others. That's an extremely important point. Write the email in such a way that your DI can forward it to others.

Implementing the Recap Email Strategy

When using the Recap Email *Sell Different!* strategy, the first key to success is the timing of your email. Send it the same day as the meeting or first thing the morning after. Remember, so much information is thrown at your DI, this email keeps your deal in the forefront of his mind.

The email should have five sections, using a bullet-point format, as shown below:

> ■ **Your Objectives**—List the challenges they shared, the objectives they have, and their reasons for needing to address them. Highlight who is impacted by those issues and the actions that have been taken to address them. You can almost see the DIs nodding as they read their words in your email. Never bad-mouth the competition, especially in writing, but rather show empathy to the DI for their current frustrations.

Whenever possible, use the words the DI used in the meeting. This personalizes your message and makes it more impactful. This section of the email provides you with a great opportunity to demonstrate to the DI that you were listening carefully to their every word during the meeting.

> ■ **How We Can Help**—This section of the email highlights the differentiators that resonated with your DI during the meeting. For each differentiator, answer

> the following question: *Why should this matter to this DI?* Give context and meaning to each differentiator. In this section of the email, without using marketing fluff, you should also answer the question of why your company is the right one for their account.

As you can probably tell, these first two sections necessitate conducting a thorough discovery. As discussed in chapter 7, during the discovery phase, it is critical to transform their emotions to the desired ones and ask both *Horizontal* and *Vertical Questions*. Without those being asked, these sections of the email are nearly impossible to write.

> - **My To-Do List**—List the action items you committed to complete with corresponding due dates.
> - **Your To-Do List**—List the action items the DI committed to complete with corresponding due dates.
> - **Next Steps**—This section addresses the next interaction you will have with the DI and who is expected to be involved.

Mistakes in your Recap Email can turn off your Decision Influencer rather than excite him to want to work with you. Before you hit "send," check the following:

- Formatting—line and paragraph spacing.
- Spelling—especially your DI's name.
- Grammar—check for inconsistent use of tenses, subject-verb agreement, and punctuation.
- Industry acronyms—write out full expressions the first time you refer to the acronym just in case the DI does not recall what it stands for.
- Slang/Jargon—avoid using these expressions as it can make you and your company look unprofessional.

Sample Recap Email Message

Here is a sample Recap Email based on Ben's meeting with Eric.

Good afternoon, Eric

Thank you for taking the time to meet with me today. I appreciate you sharing with me the objectives you have for your operations department. I'm sorry you are having these challenges and am confident we can quickly resolve those issues for you. I've put together this email to summarize the conversation we had.

Your Objectives
- Each of your locations needs to operate at a minimum of 92.8 percent efficiency to achieve desired profitability levels.
- The current systems are operating at 78.4 percent efficiency, which has caused a major impact on the division's profitability.
- Despite numerous requests, the current provider has been unable to resolve the performance issues.
- The goal is to have this issue resolved within ninety days and begin achieving desired profitability numbers.

How We Can Help
- For more than thirty years, our company has helped manufacturers improve profitability through our NPX system.
- Our NPX system has been proven to consistently provide 94.2 percent efficiency, which helps drive profitability for our clients.
- We train and certify operators in the proper use of the technology as this is critical to receiving the desired results.

- The NPX system fully integrates with your financial system to feed data for cost and performance analyses.
- Our step-by-step client onboarding program guides the transition from your current system to the NPX system over a thirty-day period. When we meet again, I'll explain our client onboarding program in detail.

My To-Do List

- Gather our list of specifications for the device we discussed and email them to you by September 1.
- Send three sample devices to you for review by August 29.

Your To-Do List

- Email me a list of your operations locations by August 28.
- Request your current operations cost for the equipment from your CFO for review at our next meeting.
- Invite Shayna Austin and Ethan Judge to our next meeting.

Next Steps

- We will meet at your office, including Shayna and Ethan, on Friday, September 10 at 2:00 p.m. to review our respective action lists. Joseph Rivera, Director of Client Onboarding, will join us to review our client onboarding program. Together, we will also brainstorm potential solutions with you and your team.

I believe this covers everything discussed during our meeting. Please let me know if I've missed anything. I look forward to seeing you, Shayna, and Ethan on September 10.

Regards,

Ben

Results You Can Have from This Strategy

"Wow! You're suggesting I do this after every meeting? That's a lot of work. Who has that kind of time?" I am sure that's what you are thinking after reading the sample Recap Email. Yes, there is work involved when implementing the Recap Email *Sell Different!* strategy. I make no apologies for that. If you see this strategy through the lens of tedious work, you'll never implement it. However, if you see it through the lens of a deal investment that helps you *Sell Different!*, you will send one of these emails after every discovery meeting.

> If you see this strategy through the lens of tedious work, you'll never implement it.

If you commit to this strategy, you will experience several benefits to help you win more deals at the prices you want.

- Decision Influencers want to work with salespeople who make them feel special, who show genuine interest in their account. No one wants to feel like they're "the sales call of the day." This email demonstrates genuine interest. Don't you think your DI knows it took time to put this email together? I bet they do. And your time investment in their account will matter to them. Since most salespeople don't send Recap Emails, your DIs will be impressed by your level of professionalism.
- You may be in a competitive situation as DIs are looking at multiple options for their account. Consider this. You provided this Recap Email and the other salespeople did not (unless they read this book).
- Little things matter in sales. Think about the deals you won and lost. When you won, you didn't blow the competition out of the water. When you lost, they didn't blow you out of the

water. With fierce competition, differentiators can be subtle and, in some cases, hard to position. How you pursue an account establishes an expectation of how you will handle the account if it is awarded to you. The Recap Email is a creative way to stand out from the other salespeople pursuing this deal.

■ Often, sales cycles become protracted because DIs do not recall the meeting as well as the salespeople do. The Recap Email reminds them of their challenges/objectives, why they are interested in working with you, what you committed to do, and what they committed to do. This strategy helps to avoid the "DI memory pitfall" that so many deals fall into. It keeps your deal moving forward.

Is the Recap Email worth the effort? Only if you want to differentiate yourself and win deals at the prices you want. I assure you that your DIs will appreciate the emails, respond to them, and it will help you stand out from the competition.

RECAP EMAIL *SELL DIFFERENT!* CONCEPT

Recap Emails demonstrate genuine interest in an account, help you stand out from the competition, and keep your deal on track.

CHAPTER 12

ARE YOU ABOUT TO LOSE
YOUR LARGEST ACCOUNT?

For the past five years, a hardware supplier sold screws to a national home building company. Whenever the home builder ordered screws, the supplier delivered them accurately and on time. If the home builder wanted Phillips screws, the supplier delivered them. If they wanted flathead screws, the supplier provided those too. The supplier had screws of all types and sizes available, which allowed them to serve this national home builder client well.

The supplier was proud of its performance with regard to the account, and the home builder was pleased with the supplier's customer service responsiveness. Over the years, this client grew to become the largest, most profitable client in the hardware supplier's portfolio. The salesperson who managed the account never worried about hitting his annual quota because of the performance of this account. He also made a small fortune in commissions on the revenue from this deal.

The home building company was thrilled with the hardware supplier's inventory management and delivery performance. The hardware supplier was delighted with the account based on its volume and profitability. The salesperson was euphoric. It made him into a company hero. This account was what you might call a textbook deal. Or was it?

One day, everything changed. Without notice, the home builder stopped buying screws from this supplier. The supplier's inventory management hadn't degraded, nor had its delivery performance. The pricing had not changed either. The salesperson still had a healthy relationship with his contacts. This seemed like a blissful relationship, but it was now gone. What happened?

In short, a competitor came along and took the account away. Despite the supplier's performance, the account was gone for good. How could this have happened given the performance of the hardware supplier?

Tactical Product Pusher to Strategic Solution Provider

The competitor used a *Sell Different!* strategy to win the deal at the prices they wanted. Their salesperson didn't pursue the account with the old-fashioned sales approach of offering to save them a nickel on each order. Besides, that strategy probably would not have worked given the supplier's performance with the account.

The competitor's salesperson talked with a senior executive of the home builder, not just about screws, but rather about their overall construction needs. That salesperson inquired about the tools used to install the screws and the material in which the screws were installed. He had a comprehensive solution conversation with the home builder. Taking a step back and reflecting on the incumbent's relationship, it was merely tactical, not strategic.

By introducing the simplicity of buying screws, tools, and materials from one supplier, this competitor sparked intrigue in the home builder. His conversation was not about price, but rather on overall cost savings that could result from the home builder consolidating its needs with a single provider. The salesperson also talked about the efficiency the home builder would gain by placing these orders with his company. And, if they ever had questions about any aspect of their orders, they would simply need to contact this one supplier. In essence, the competitor positioned a business case for supplier consolidation, and it worked fabulously.

Here is the real shame of this situation. The incumbent supplier offered tools and materials just like the new supplier. They could have provided a comprehensive solution rather than a single product, but they never had the conversation with the home builder. This account should not have been lost. After all, the incumbent supplier offered everything the competitor offered. But now it was too late.

The incumbent supplier's salesperson was afraid to be perceived by the home builder as greedy and didn't want to risk jeopardizing his relationships. He and his company were happy with the account's revenue and profitability. They believed that because of their strong inventory management and delivery, they had the account "locked up" forever and no one would be able to take it away from them. Consequently, they grew complacent. Unfortunately for them, they were dead wrong! Account complacency proved to be their Achilles' heel.

Again, this competitor didn't take the account away by "dropping its drawers" on price. They positioned the value of supplier consolidation with a comprehensive solution that made a strong business case justifying a change. The incumbent was merely a product pusher and did not do enough to provide meaningful, differentiated value.

Conquer Accounts Strategy

This story parallels a dynamic I find in most companies. They have a fragmented client portfolio. The portfolio resembles a slice of Swiss cheese with big holes in it everywhere. They sell a product (or two) to a client, but they don't develop a strategy to position the full solution their company can deliver. They may have sold a single product to a company or a full solution to a division or a single location of a company. In these cases, there is more selling to be done, and lots of it!

This isn't just a business-to-business sales issue. It affects consumer selling as well. If you sell carpet cleaning, window cleaning, and deck power washing, you could have the same Swiss cheese dynamic in your client portfolio. You may have sold one of those services to a homeowner, but you did not sell the full suite that your company offers. That means a competitor, who introduces the benefits of a sole provider for those services, can take that account away from you, the same way the hardware supplier's competitor took their client away from them.

> It should be a punishable sales crime when an account is lost to a competitor who sold your client the same solution you could have offered, but never did.

This leads me to share with you my Conquer Accounts *Sell Different!* strategy. This strategy introduces new revenue opportunities and removes account vulnerabilities. The new opportunities come in the form of increased revenue by selling additional products and services to existing clients. Vulnerabilities are eliminated because you move from being a tactical product pusher to a strategic solution provider.

Here is the core Conquer Accounts *Sell Different!* strategy question to ask yourself about each of your clients:

> **"What else are they buying that we offer, but they are not currently buying from us?"**

I'm suggesting you contrast what your company offers with what your clients are already buying, but from your competitors. The story I shared about the hardware supplier was really a colossal sales failure. It should be a punishable sales crime when an account is lost to a competitor who sold your client the same solution you could have offered, but never did. This sales mistake is avoidable and should never happen.

Changing gears to the positive side of the equation, a Conquer Accounts *Sell Different!* strategy can have an exponential impact on growth. According to some client portfolios I have analyzed, moving clients from a tactical product relationship to a strategic solution relationship by implementing a well-executed Conquer Accounts strategy could increase company revenue tenfold.

If you are a salesperson reading this, it may seem like you need the company to adopt this strategy to begin using it. Not true! Have you ever looked at your client portfolio and asked yourself how much untapped revenue it represents? If you haven't, you should. There is no reason why you can't implement this strategy right now without receiving a directive from the company. Analyze your client portfolio to find its opportunities and vulnerabilities. Don't wait for your sales manager to tell you to do it. By then, you could be too late. The unnecessary holes in your portfolio mean you leave revenue on the table and open the door to the competition.

> Have you ever looked at your client portfolio and asked yourself how much untapped revenue it represents?

Acquiring new clients is considered the fun part of sales. It's "high fives" all around when a salesperson adds a new logo to the client portfolio even when it is merely a tactical product sale. The most celebrated win should occur when a Conquer Accounts *Sell Different!* strategy is successfully deployed, leading to significantly more revenue recognized and vulnerabilities removed.

Coming back to the story, the incumbent supplier's salesperson was afraid to have a conversation with the home builder about expanding the relationship because he didn't want to be seen as an opportunist. That cost him dearly. He was afraid to "upset the applecart" by trying to sell them more and risk his fat commission checks. Quite frankly, this salesperson provided a disservice to his client. By not talking with them about the opportunities associated with supplier consolidation, they incurred unnecessary inefficiencies and costs. This strategy does not jeopardize commission checks, but burying your head in the sand and hoping the competitors don't take the account away does.

■ ■ ■

The Conquering Accounts Master

There is one company that uses the Conquer Accounts *Sell Different!* strategy better than any company I've ever seen, but they don't call it that. The company is Amazon. For every product on their website, they have created a fully connected sales web designed to increase the size of your purchase, and they do it in a positive, helpful way. Based on the item you are about to buy, Amazon provides suggestions of other products you may want in conjunction with that item. "Oh yeah, I need that too."

As I wrote this chapter, I went on the Amazon website and searched for screws. In the "frequently bought together" section, they offered me both drills and drill bits. Amazon isn't just satisfied with selling you the product you searched for; they want to sell you a full solution. While it may seem like corporate greed, that is not how their clientele see it. They perceive Amazon as being helpful and making it easy for them to accomplish their objectives, while Amazon increases revenue.

How to Identify Opportunities and Remove Vulnerabilities from Your Client Portfolio

Chances are, what you are selling isn't as robust as what Amazon offers, which means you won't have a Conquer Accounts technological solution as strong as theirs. Your first step should be to manually assemble a Conquer Accounts–Product Contrast Matrix that helps you identify the opportunities and vulnerabilities in your account portfolio. Here's how:

1. Lay out a page in landscape format and insert a table with six columns.

2. Label the following columns:
   - Product
   - Competition
   - Market Segment/
     Decision Influencer
   - Related Products/
     Services
   - Synergy
   - Competition for
     Related Products

3. In the first column (Product), list all the products your
   company offers.

4. In the second column (Competition), list all the competitors
   that offer the same (or similar) product as the one listed.

5. In the third column (Market Segment/Decision Influencer),
   identify which market segments and DIs buy this particular
   product.

6. In the fourth column (Related Products/Services), list all the
   products/services you sell that a client who bought what you
   listed in the first column would also need. For example, if the
   listed product is a screw, this is the section where you would
   include screwdrivers, drills, drill bits, and materials in which
   screws would be used.

   Ask yourself, *"If they are buying this product, what other products of ours should also be of interest?"* This "money column" of the
   Conquer Accounts–Product Contrast Matrix is a manual way
   to incorporate the same automated strategy Amazon uses when
   they show you "Frequently Bought Together." If the incumbent
   hardware supplier had asked themselves this question, they
   would have found opportunities on both sides of the screw.

7. In the fifth column (Synergy), identify why those other
   products should be of interest by asking yourself, *"What is the
   synergy between the product they are currently buying and the
   related ones?"* In the case of screws, the purchasers may need
   tools and materials.

8. In the sixth column (Competition for Related Products), list
   the competitors who come into play when positioning related

products. This list, which may or may not be the same as the second column, is important to identify as part of the selling strategy.

Once you have assembled your Conquer Accounts–Product Contrast Matrix, the next step is to compare it with your client portfolio. This exercise exposes the Swiss cheese holes in your accounts. However, now you have the tools to take action on them. The Matrix helps you see the opportunities and vulnerabilities in the portfolio.

If you are a salesperson, develop both a strategy and timeline to pursue each opportunity and remove each vulnerability.

If you are a sales manager/executive, take the following actions:

1. Run the Conquer Accounts–Product Contrast Matrix analysis for your entire account portfolio.
2. Based on the results, assign a salesperson to each account to address the opportunities and vulnerabilities.
3. Prioritize the accounts based on the size of the opportunities and vulnerabilities.
4. Work with the salespeople to develop both a strategy and a timeline to implement it.
5. Develop a report with the following columns to address the strategy:
   - Account Name.
   - Assigned Salesperson.
   - What the Account Currently Buys from Us.
   - What the Account Should Be Buying from Us.
   - Who the Account Is Buying That Item from Today.
   - The Strategy to Position Consolidation with Us.
   - Date by Which the Salesperson Will Have Positioned Consolidation.

Salespeople frequently toss out the expression "one-stop shop" as a strategy to position supplier consolidation when initially selling their products and services. That message can be compelling, leading DIs to buy one item today, with future purchasing needs in mind.

While they may hear that message today, it is likely they will forget about it over time. It is the salesperson's responsibility to keep the supplier consolidation message in the forefront of the DIs' minds and work with them to take advantage of the opportunities that it affords. By doing so, you avoid the peril that led to the demise of the hardware supplier's relationship with the home builder.

CONQUER ACCOUNTS *SELL DIFFERENT!* CONCEPT

By focusing on selling the full range of capabilities your company offers, vulnerabilities are removed and revenue from your client portfolio increases.

CHAPTER 13

CUSTOMER SERVICE IS NOT ACCOUNT MANAGEMENT

I n chapter 12, I shared the story of a hardware supplier who was outsold by a competitor. That competitor successfully leveraged a Conquer Accounts *Sell Different!* strategy to take the client away from the incumbent. Yet, when we think about why the incumbent was vulnerable to the competition, there's another perspective to consider.

Two commonly used phrases are "Customer Service" and "Account Management." Executives and salespeople frequently use these terms interchangeably. Customer service and account management are both functions in which many people in your organization can be involved. But they are not the same thing. Let's explore the difference.

Customer Service occurs whenever clients request something from you. They place an order, call your call center, or send an email expressing a need. In these cases, the measurement of success is responsiveness, defined as accuracy and timeliness. In some cases, responsiveness can be a differentiator for you, particularly when a competitor provides inadequate customer service. Because no salesperson ever describes their company as being weak in customer service, your challenge is to prove to a Decision Influencer that your customer service is superior. Every salesperson preaches that they deliver the best customer service experience in the world, and many offer testimonials from clients as proof of it.

To demonstrate the customer service function, I'll use an example that all of us have experienced: dining in a nice restaurant. When you go to a restaurant, you expect the waitstaff to tend to your table shortly after you sit down. You don't expect to wait twenty minutes to be served water and bread or given a menu. You also don't expect it to take that long for the waitstaff to visit your table and take your order.

When you place the food order, you expect that your meal will be delivered accurately and in a timely fashion. After the meal, you expect the check to be calculated correctly. When all these tasks are performed as expected, diners refer to this as a "great customer service experience." However, these aspects are merely *table stakes*. We expect that all of these services will be delivered flawlessly during every dining experience. When any of them are faulty, diners refer to the issues as "poor customer service."

Good customer service is not "going above and beyond" what is expected to delight the diner. While it is true that many businesses struggle with the basics, relying on customer service to retain your clientele is a flawed strategy, as that hardware supplier learned.

Delivering customer service well can keep a client from looking for an alternative supplier, but it won't stop a competitor from swooping in, creating intrigue, and taking the account away. To eliminate that vulnerability and retain your clients, you will need an Account Management *Sell Different!* strategy.

Account Management is the converse of customer service. Whereas customer service is considered to be a responsive function, *account management* is proactive. Account Management *Sell Different!* strategy is the prescriptive value you deliver to your clients above and beyond the benefit your products or services provide. Notice the use of the word "prescriptive." The perception of meaningful value does not happen accidentally. It is by design. It is intended by you as part of the overall client experience with your company. The core purpose of the account management function is to create client delight leading to increased tenure, revenue, and profit for your company. Prescribing, or defining, the account management experience will lead to these outcomes.

Over the years, I have found companies expend a tremendous amount of energy in acquiring new clients. Not enough attention is paid to developing strategies for increasing client retention and growth. Executives don't invest enough time in Account Management *Sell Different!* strategy. I find that most organizations offer nothing more than a basic A, B, C classification of clients ranked only by recognized revenue. A beautiful document presenting these client rankings will be distributed throughout the organization with no strategy included and no expectations set. All the team hears is, "This is the ranking of our A, B, and C clients." Of course, no one knows what to do with that information, so it doesn't drive any prescriptive, proactive behaviors. There is nothing wrong with having an A, B, C ranking. The problem is when there is no definition of what each ranking category means.

> The core purpose of the account management function is to create client delight leading to increased tenure, revenue, and profit for your company.

Executives and salespeople often use the expression "valued partner" to describe their client relationships. Solid customer service is what a vendor provides, but this alone will not create a perception of meaningful value and does not lead you to be seen as a partner. Strong account management is the way for clients to see you as the valued partner that they need and desire.

While executives preach the importance of account management strategy to the team, typically no one defines it or formulates a plan to do it methodically. Most important, companies miss out on this Account Management *Sell Different!* strategy opportunity to acquire, retain, and grow clients. "Wait a minute! Did he say *acquire* clients through account management?" Absolutely! When you have a prescriptive account management program, that becomes a topic of conversation when wooing new clients. Account management is your way of delivering meaningful value beyond the benefits of what you sell. This is a great way to differentiate yourself from your competitors.

Analyzing Your Client Portfolio

Some companies rank their clients exclusively by recognized revenue. Others don't rank them at all. Ranking clients is a key task every company should perform, and the approach must be something more than simply recognized revenue classification. Why is this so important? Without a sophisticated method for ranking clients, some will be underserved while others will be overserved by your company.

The initial step in the development of your Account Management *Sell Different!* strategy is to rank your client portfolio in a meaningful way. Client rankings should be assembled after conducting my "Five-Point Client Value Analysis" of your overall book of business.

The **first point** of the analysis is "Recognized Revenue." This is where the evaluation begins, but it does not depict the complete picture. Consider this: What if a company spends $1 million annually on widgets, and your widget-making company has only 1 percent of that spend? At that spend level, the 1 percent would rank them low on your scale. Given their potential for significantly more revenue, do you really want to treat them like a small client?

The **second point** to analyze is "Wallet Share Percentage." That is the portion of the client spend your company receives versus the total possible if they were to consolidate their account with your company. It represents the potential revenue the account could generate if your company had it all.

Wallet share percentage is not always easy to determine and is often incalculable. That means an educated guess is often used for this segment of the analysis. Low wallet share percentage is best addressed using the Conquer Accounts *Sell Different!* strategy described in chapter 12. That strategy could turn a mediocre revenue account into one of the largest clients in your portfolio.

The **third point** to analyze is "Account Profitability." Some clients may generate substantial revenue for your company, but the margin on that revenue is low. Yet, a mid-sized revenue client may be significantly more profitable. Without taking account profitability into consideration in the analysis, recognized revenue can create a false impression of client value in the portfolio. There are numerous instances in which the largest clients are the worst clients in the portfolio based on account profitability.

Making matters worse, these accounts are provided with account management services at the highest levels, which further dilutes their profitability. The high level of account management is delivered, in this case, for the sole reason that no one considered account profitability when providing those services.

The **fourth point** to consider is "Strategic Account." Some clients may only be capable of generating a smidgeon of revenue although you possess 100 percent of their wallet share. However, having them in your client portfolio helps you establish credibility with prospective clients. It could be their name, brand, market segment, or a specialized solution you deployed for them that creates value to your organization beyond the client's revenue contribution. This is a strategic account that benefits your company beyond recognized revenue or the potential of more dollars. Looking at this client from the vantage points of recognized revenue or revenue potential would lead you to classify them low in the ranking. Do you really want to treat a strategic account like a miniscule client?

The **fifth point** to consider is the "Pain Factor." These are clients who are tremendously burdensome for your company to support. Perhaps they generate significant revenue, but it is painful to support the account. Maybe your company doesn't have the technology or systems needed to handle them properly, which means they are out of alignment with your strengths. Or their people are extremely difficult to deal with. This is another important consideration when ranking clients.

Developing a Meaningful Ranking System

With each of the "Five-Point Client Value Analysis" components in mind, the next step is to develop a system to appropriately rank each client. The system is intended to categorize clients based on their value to your organization. While you are probably looking for a simple mathematical equation that tells you how to rank your clients, one is not forthcoming. The ranking requires scrutiny beyond calculation.

Start your ranking based on client value by dividing your client portfolio into three categories, A, B, and C. While there isn't a mathematical equation to calculate client value, here are the considerations to keep in mind:

- **For recognized revenue**—rank each client high, medium, or low based on the amount of revenue your company receives from that client. The top 10 percent should be ranked "high," the next 10 percent should be ranked "medium," and the remaining 80 percent should be ranked "low." This is based on the commonly known concept that 80 percent of revenue is generated by 20 percent of your clients.
- **For wallet share percentage**—rank each client high, medium, or low based on the spend percentage your company has for the client. "High"-ranking clients are those for which you have control of more than 75 percent of their wallet share. "Medium"-ranking clients are those for which you have between 50 and 75 percent of their wallet share. "Low"-ranking clients are those for which you have less than 50 percent of their wallet share.
- **For account profitability**—rank each client high, medium, or low based on the margin generated. Every company has its own parameters for expected margin, so it is not possible to give you a fixed number for this section. However, "high" rankings are to be assigned to those clients who generate the desired margins on the generated revenue. "Medium" rankings are to be assigned to clients who generate acceptable margins on the generated revenue. "Low" rankings are to be assigned to clients who generate unacceptable margins on the generated revenue.

- **For strategic account**—removing both revenue and profit considerations, rank each client based on the value it represents for your business. This takes into consideration their name or brand recognition or a particular solution deployed. "High" rankings are to be assigned to those clients who are considered high value. "Medium" rankings are to be assigned to those clients who are considered medium value. "Low" rankings are to be assigned to those clients whose name, brand recognition, market segment, or the solution deployed do not provide any additional value for your company.

- **For the pain factor**—consider what is involved in supporting this client. Are their needs in alignment with the areas in which your company excels? How difficult is it to make this client happy? "Low" rankings are to be assigned to those clients who are in alignment with where your company excels and are easy to support. "Medium" rankings are to be assigned to those clients who are also in alignment with where your company excels but are more challenging to support. "High" rankings are to be assigned to those clients who are not in alignment with where your company excels or are extremely difficult to please.

Based on the "Five-Point Client Value Analysis," plot your accounts in a matrix. List the clients' names in the left-hand column. List the five points of the analysis as column headers. The seventh column should be titled "Overall Client Ranking." It is in this column that you will consider the results of the "Five-Point Client Value Analysis" and give each client an overall ranking of A, B, or C.

Given the five points, how do you set an overall ranking for each client? The answer to that question is yet another question:

What level of account management service do you want to offer the client?

Some factors to consider when developing your overall client ranking:

- **Recognized Revenue relative to Wallet Share Percentage—** Consider the likelihood of increasing the wallet share percentage and the impact on the account's recognized revenue. If growth is likely and it would lead to significantly more revenue, that's an important factor to consider in the overall client ranking.
- **Recognized Revenue relative to Account Profitability—** While the percentage might not be at the desired level, the volume of profit dollars may be significant to your business. That can be a factor that leads you to elevate their overall client ranking.
- **Strategic Account—**An account that receives a "high" ranking as a Strategic Account should receive an "A" or "B" in your overall client ranking.
- **Pain Factor relative to Account Profitability—**An account with a "high" ranking for pain factor and a "low" ranking for account profitability should be considered for removal from your portfolio. That is most often a bad account for your business.

A common misperception is that account management is comprised of a fixed level of service for all clients to receive. Many companies handle the function that way. Yet, there should be tiers of account management services offered based on the results of the "Five-Point Client Value Analysis." Your "A" clients should not receive the same level of account management service as your "C" clients.

Account management is an investment your company makes in client relationships.

Account management is an investment your company makes in client relationships. That investment is a function of how you define each client's value.

Defining the Account Management Experience

What was the point of the ranking exercise that I just described? Was it to create a "prettier" version of your client rankings? No. The purpose of the "Five-Point Client Value Analysis" ranking is to determine the appropriate levels of account management services to be provided based on client value.

Certainly, no client should be neglected and receive no account management services. If you don't want the account (high pain factor), fire the client. Every client in your portfolio should be treated well, but not in the same fashion. Account management is a cost to your business. You cannot afford to provide the same level to every client, nor should you want to.

> Every client in your portfolio should be treated well, but not in the same fashion.

But what prescribed account management experience will you provide to your clients? Let's revisit the core purpose of account management: to create client delight, leading to increased tenure, revenue, and profit for your company. Here are some options to include in your account management program.

- **Executive sponsorship**—A member of the executive team is assigned to the account and tasked with developing high-level client relationships. It is commonly offered to "A" clients. For "B" clients, a management team member can be assigned as a sponsor. Usually, "C" clients are not assigned a sponsor.
- **Meetings**—Based on the A, B, C ranking system, determine the number of times you will meet with each classification of client and for what purpose. The number of meetings among the three types should not be uniform. There should be consideration for whether the meetings will be conducted in person or virtually. Also, think about location of the meetings. Based on the ranking, you may want to invite certain clients to

meet at your corporate offices (rather than theirs) for account reviews and planning sessions. Some companies offer to pay travel expenses for their "A" clients to visit their facilities.

■ **New product/feature access**—As your company introduces new products/features to the marketplace, you can provide access to them based on your client ranking system. Higher-ranked clients should receive access before other clients.

■ **Account monitoring**—For your "A" clients, their performance should be carefully tracked and monitored by a member of your team who will keep an eye on the account, its purchasing patterns, and news.

■ **Focus group/advisory board invitations**—These are sessions established to brainstorm new products or services. Involvement with focus groups and advisory boards strengthens client relationships. These invitations should be extended to "A" and sometimes "B" clients.

■ **Data analyses**—Any vendor can generate a report and email it to a DI. Want them to see you as a trusted advisor, a valued partner? Analyze the report. Share with your clients what the data tells you. Ask questions based on the data, share recommendations, and help your clients arrive at informed decisions. This allows you to demonstrate expertise and provides the best solution they can have from you for the dollars they are willing to invest.

■ **Newsletters**—You can easily create these using online tools. Newsletters keep clients informed of industry happenings, regulatory news, best practices, and trends. The goal is not to peddle your wares, but to provide value that helps them in their roles. Newsletters should be sent to all clients, regardless of ranking.

This is just a small sampling of the account management options available to you. Based on your business, your options will differ. The key is to fully define the account management experience you want to provide based on your overall client ranking. This allows you to deliver meaningful value beyond what your product offers. Account Management *Sell Different!* strategy helps you retain and grow your existing clients while you win more deals at the prices you want.

ACCOUNT MANAGEMENT *SELL DIFFERENT!* CONCEPT

Account management is the proactive, prescriptive value offered to your clients, above and beyond the benefits of what you sell, to create client delight resulting in increased tenure, revenue, and profit.

CHAPTER 14

THE GIFT EVERY SALESPERSON HAS BEEN GIVEN

A fun question I like to ask salespeople is: "What is a salesperson's most productive day of the year?" I hear answers like "Tuesdays," "the last day of the month," and "the first day of the year." None of these answers are even close to being correct. So,

"What is a salesperson's most productive day of the year?"

Time Investment

The most productive day of the year for salespeople is the day before they go on vacation. Imagine it's the day before you head out on a weeklong getaway. Every task sitting in front of you goes through a filtering process to determine what needs to be done now, what can wait, and what should not be completed by you at all.

That day, you are laser-focused on completing just those tasks before you walk out the door. You even have a punch list and mark each one completed.

As the day ends, not only are you excited anticipating your time away, but you feel a strong sense of accomplishment. And you should! Not one minute of that day was wasted. You carefully selected everything you would do during those minutes. You, and you alone, controlled the day.

What if you had that same degree of focus every day of your selling career? How much could you exponentially increase your success simply by challenging yourself to better manage the clock? We all have exactly the same number of minutes each day. The difference between top performers and mediocre ones is determined by how those minutes are invested. Once a minute has passed, it's gone forever. Nothing we do will ever bring that time back to us.

> The difference between top performers and mediocre ones is determined by how those minutes are invested.

How you invest your time, every single day, determines your future success. That means you need to make a conscious decision to use every minute of every day. No one ever wants to look back and say to themselves, "I wish I did . . ." To avoid experiencing that regret, have a plan to manage both time and tasks.

In the sales profession, you can be extremely busy all day long but accomplish little. You go home exhausted after a full day, but as you reflect on it, you realize you did nothing to increase your sales. Since increasing sales is at the core of a salesperson's responsibilities, it means the day was a total loss.

Success is easily quantifiable in the sales profession. There is a myriad of data, available in most companies, that depicts those salespeople who are successful and those who are not. Certainly, goal attainment is one of those data points. One of those metrics is *not* "who worked the hardest." In sales, no one cares how hard you work. There are no awards for the hardest-working salesperson. Metrics are associated with goal attainment and the various phases of new client acquisition or growth. Working hard, by itself, does not make salespeople successful. But working smart does.

The First Task That "Goes Out the Window"

What is the first task that gets cast aside when salespeople get "busy"? *Prospecting!* Most salespeople dread this task. I placed quotation marks around "busy" because some salespeople make themselves busy to avoid prospecting. After all, hearing "no" all day long is exhausting, frustrating, and painful. That's why it's the first task that is skipped when other ones arise. While at the time, you may feel great having skipped the pain of prospecting, you will experience agony weeks and months later when your pipeline is as dry as the Sahara Desert.

To keep prospecting in the forefront of your mind, I'll share with you a Priority Management *Sell Different!* strategy. Just as you would for any other important appointment, create fixed appointments in your calendar for your prospecting sessions. Each session should be no longer than two hours, which will allow you to stay sharp throughout. After two hours, fatigue sets in for many salespeople, so they become less effective, which is why I recommend this limited duration.

During these sessions, do not read emails or texts; do not answer phone calls either. Set aside this time strictly for outbound prospecting activities and nothing else. The only two permissible activities are creating/sending prospecting emails and making outbound phone calls. That's it. Put your phone on "do not disturb," stay out of your email inbox, and concentrate on this critical activity.

Here's the key to making these sessions super productive: *have your pursuit list prepared before you start.* These sessions are not times to research and think about whom to contact. This is time for outbound emails and outbound phone calls only.

Sure, you may get "busy," but prospecting sessions are never to be canceled. They can be rescheduled during the same week if there is a significant conflict such as a client meeting. Top salespeople don't cancel prospecting sessions; they find a way to make them happen. If you push it off until the future, the same thing will happen with your success. And no one wants to put off receiving fat commission checks!

Doctor Task Management

Ever notice when you go to the doctor that, when the doctor enters the consultation room, she is fully prepared to meet with you? A receptionist scheduled the appointment, documented your insurance information, and processed your payment afterward. A nurse captured your medical history, took your blood pressure, and weighed you. The time the doctor spent with you was extremely focused because she had been provided with all that data before she walked in.

Doctors don't weigh patients because it is a waste of their time given their high level of skills. They recognize the value of time and focus on their revenue per minute. They only perform tasks that necessitate their specialized skill set. Their objective is to have a productive consultation with a patient using the fewest minutes possible. Of course, they don't make a patient feel rushed, but they do effectively use their resources to manage the overall patient experience.

While doctors don't weigh patients, receptionists don't diagnose patients because they don't have the credentials or expertise to do so. Each employee in the practice is assigned specific tasks within their expertise and scope of responsibilities. A medical office has tremendous clarity on who handles which tasks. This clarity is often missing in other business settings.

What if we took that same task management approach with sales? In this model, the "doctor" is the salesperson who will be expected to perform only those tasks that require her expertise. The "nurse" and "receptionist" are others in the organization who can perform necessary tasks that don't require the level of skill a salesperson possesses. Those other tasks need to be completed, but the "doctor" should not be the one completing them.

The core purpose of salespeople, the reason they are on the payroll, is to generate revenue. Sometimes, however, management loses sight of that purpose and assigns tasks to salespeople that distract them from revenue generation. This is not just a management issue. Salespeople are often guilty as well. They will voluntarily take on tasks that they should not be doing. It's understandable because, after all, practically anything is more fun than prospecting.

Salespeople who have been with an organization for a long time often fall into this trap. Since they know how to solve client problems, they handle these issues themselves, rather than let the "nurse" and "receptionist" take care of them. Sure, salespeople feel a sense of accomplishment because they fixed the problem, but at what cost to their future sales success? Handling client problems themselves means they didn't invest time on "doctor" tasks. Unfortunately, those minutes are lost forever.

Salespeople who get involved with client issues that others should be addressing create a client-problem vacuum. Since everyone in the company knows that these salespeople will resolve the issues, they pass them to the salespeople. When this happens, the "doctor" is performing "nurse" and "receptionist" functions. This is costly to the organization because at that moment no one is performing "doctor" tasks.

For outside salespeople stuck in this never-ending cycle, I suggest you should not be in the office. If you aren't available, the organization is forced to resolve these issues without your involvement. If you can't get away from the office, push back on those tasks in an appropriate fashion and keep them off your plate.

Management has a responsibility to ensure that every "doctor" minute associated with their salespeople is wisely invested.

Management has a responsibility to ensure that every "doctor" minute associated with their salespeople is wisely invested. Management also has a responsibility to oversee the "doctors" and make sure they don't fall into the "nurse" and "receptionist" trap. When that happens, salespeople are transformed into expensive client service representatives. "Doctors" need to concentrate on their most important, valuable tasks, which are revenue-related. If the "doctors" aren't generating revenue for the company, no one is!

Sales Task Optimization

To avoid the missteps associated with "doctors" performing "nurse" and "receptionist" tasks, make a list of all the responsibilities associated with new client acquisition, retention, and growth. Start from the beginning of prospecting and address all duties through customer service and account management. Here is a sample task list:

- Develop prospect lists for pursuit.
- Research prospects.
- Strategically analyze potential opportunities.
- Strategically analyze current clients.
- Develop account pursuit strategies.
- Make outbound prospecting calls.
- Generate leads.
- Identify potential lead partners.
- Foster relationships with lead partners.
- Conduct business development functions with industry partners.
- Participate in trade-show booth activities.
- Receive inbound leads.
- Upsell existing clients.
- Cross-sell existing clients.
- Generate referral leads.
- Schedule discovery meetings.
- Conduct discovery meetings.
- Develop solutions for prospective clients.
- Develop group presentations for prospects.
- Modify group presentations for DIs.
- Deliver group presentations to DIs.
- Host DI visits.
- Host client visits.
- Conduct system demonstrations.

- Resolve deal obstacles (concerns, objections, stalls).
- Take the lead on deals.
- Write proposals.
- Handle reference requests.
- Develop pricing.
- Respond to Requests for Proposals (RFPs).
- Create accounts in the CRM.
- Update accounts in the CRM.
- Forecast deals in the CRM.
- Manage the new client onboarding process.
- Set up new clients in the system.
- Provide customer service functions.
- Provide account management functions.
- Conduct profitability analyses with clients.
- Create invoices.
- Send invoices.
- Manage client receivables.
- Conduct competitor analyses.
- Book travel.
- Complete commission reports.
- Create client case studies.
- Develop a list of references.

With the master list developed, the next step is to assign tasks to the "doctor," "nurse," and "receptionist." It is possible that a task may be assigned to more than one role, but that should be the exception, not the norm.

- "Doctor" tasks are those requiring the *highest* level of sales/technical knowledge and skill.
- "Nurse" tasks are those requiring a *moderate* level of sales/technical knowledge and skill.
- "Receptionist" tasks are those requiring the *lowest* level of sales/technical knowledge and skill.

While I referenced the "doctor" being the salesperson, that is not always the case. One of my clients uses a virtual selling approach where the "doctor" is their solution engineer. They have junior-level salespeople whose primary responsibility is to generate qualified meetings for their solution engineer to work his magic. For them, the solution engineer is the one whose minutes are most valuable and whose time needs to be carefully managed. That means he needs to be able to "walk" from virtual room to virtual room all day long. He should be fully prepared for the meeting by the salespeople to be able to conduct an effective meeting in the fewest minutes possible.

If you are a manager reading this section, I encourage you to assign the tasks for the entire organization and share the plan with the teams. This ensures everyone has clarity concerning their primary responsibilities relative to new client acquisition, retention, and growth. While the medical metaphor is helpful to assemble this plan, I would not recommend sharing that approach with the entire organization. Those considered "nurse" or "receptionist" in the matrix could be offended as they feel they are seen as less important than "doctors." The key output from the exercise is a clear understanding of who is expected to do what.

If you are a salesperson reading this section, challenge yourself with that task list and hold yourself accountable for the tasks that necessitate your involvement. The company's management team may have assigned you "nurse" or "doctor" tasks. However, there are often cases when salespeople are performing tasks they should not be, and management is not aware of that issue. This exercise educates management about your sales detractors, meaning they can help you stay focused on the critical sales tasks that only you are qualified to complete.

The main purpose of Priority Management *Sell Different!* strategy is to maximize your selling minutes. Hold yourself accountable for completing the tasks that belong only to you. Let others handle the "non-you" tasks. Salespeople who use their resources wisely invest their minutes to boost performance. They are the ones who earn the most money. Let's make that person you!

PRIORITY MANAGEMENT *SELL DIFFERENT!* CONCEPT

Every minute of every day needs to be wisely invested to maximize selling time, performance, and income.

CHAPTER 15

THE MAJOR FLAW WHEN COMPARING SALESPEOPLE WITH ATHLETES

Countless articles, blog posts, and books have been written comparing salespeople to professional athletes. "Salespeople are business athletes," they say. I'm sure you have come across variations of that expression and understand why these two groups are so often compared to each other. Both have strong determination, are goal oriented, and have a burning desire to win. Yet, there is one significant difference between them that few talk about.

Professional athletes invest countless hours developing their knowledge and skills with the fundamental goal of mastery. They are seeking to become champions in their respective sport. They spend hours, days, weeks, months, and years refining and improving their craft, recognizing that having strong muscle memory is key to their success. During competition, professional athletes have no time to think. Their bodies need to perform flawlessly and at optimal levels based on the investment they made during practice. They literally have sweat equity.

Professional athletes also recognize that their competitors are getting stronger and tougher every day. If they don't also improve, the competition will leave them in the dust. They are students of the game they play. These athletes study game tape of their performances, searching for a competitive edge. They are forever looking for ways to improve.

Flawed Comparison

This is where the comparison of professional athletes and salespeople collapses. Professional athletes invest time and energy improving themselves in preparation for competition. Salespeople play the game over and over again just hoping to be better each time. This is a major difference that almost invalidates the comparison.

During my conversations with salespeople, I hear them talk about the deals they are pursuing, but rarely do I hear them talk about their efforts to become better salespeople. If they can't get in the door or they lose a deal to the competition, instead of taking it as a message to improve, they just move on to the next opportunity. I'm not suggesting that they become downtrodden when these things happen, but they should take action to advance their knowledge and skills.

One of my long-term clients is a prestigious minor league baseball team. During a summer visit to their stadium, the owner took me on a tour of the facility. It was a blazing hot day, over one hundred degrees. On the field, four catchers, in full gear, were working with coaches on blocking pitches in the dirt. They were out there all day in the blistering heat. I bet they lost ten pounds that day just from sweating.

> I have found most salespeople don't invest enough time, outside of the sales game, on improving performance.

Why would they work so hard on that skill in those tough conditions? Imagine it's the bottom of the ninth inning in a tied baseball game with the winning run on third base. The pitcher winds up and unintentionally throws the pitch in the dirt. There is no time for the catcher to think about blocking the ball. His body needs to perform automatically, or the game is lost.

During the stadium tour, we walked past the team's salespeople who were comfortably seated in an air-conditioned office. They were busy on the phones working with Decision Influencers to sell season tickets and suites. When I asked them about the time they spend "improving their game" like the players on the field, you can imagine the answer I received. It was a deafening silence.

Salespeople failing to invest in themselves is not unique to this sales team. I have found most salespeople don't invest enough time, outside of the sales game, on improving performance. Just like in sports, there are no do-overs. You "screw up" a sales call or a presentation, the game is over. You lost!

Are You a Sales Professional?

Self-made billionaire Mark Cuban (*Shark Tank* star and owner of the Dallas Mavericks basketball team) says it best: "Work like there is someone working twenty-four hours a day to take it all away from you." Certainly, that's the perspective that professional athletes have, but what about salespeople? Most don't have the sense of urgency that Cuban advocates.

I characterize a "professional" as someone who is committed to craft mastery in their chosen field. It's someone willing to invest in themselves to be the best they can be. That's what professional athletes do. But what about you? Should you be referred to as a professional salesperson? Have you earned that title? The answer is "yes" if you possess that critical desire to be the best and invest the time to achieve it, which means you are committed to Skill Development *Sell Different!* strategy.

If a professional athlete has a "gap in their game," they invest time and sweat to eliminate the weakness. Losing is awful! It's painful. Considering the number of hours a professional athlete spends preparing for competition, coming up just short of victory is unacceptable. When that happens, they go back to work. They certainly don't just wish to be better the next time. But many salespeople do exactly that. While a failure shouldn't lead them to become distraught, it should tell them they need to be better for the next one and take the steps to improve now.

Many professional athletes pay, out of their own pocket, for coaches to help take them to the next level. Not many salespeople would ever consider doing that. I've heard more than a few say, "If my company wants me to sell better, they can pay for a sales trainer." For me, hearing that is like nails on a chalkboard. The company doesn't own your success. You do! This is your career. Don't wait for your company to figure out that you need to improve. Take action and do it today! It's your paycheck.

Rob, a principal in a New York accounting firm, is a perfect example of someone who took ownership of his career. Last summer, he read my book *Sales Differentiation*. While he is an accounting practitioner, he also has business development responsibilities with which he was struggling. After reading the book, he reached out to me for further help. When we talked, he shared he was zero for eight in the deals he had pursued over a ten-month period. He also mentioned that his goal to become a partner was in jeopardy because he had not yet demonstrated mastery of new client acquisition.

In most accounting firms, if you can't generate new business, it is very difficult to rise to the level of partner. While Rob was one step away from this goal, it was still beyond his grasp. We had a conversation about the scope of a sales coaching engagement and the fee for it. To my pleasant surprise, he agreed to fund the program out of his own pocket.

Over the next three months, we developed strategies for his selling approach and practiced, practiced, practiced. As a result, success happened fast for Rob. In the months after completing the program, he won sixteen deals (and counting) at the prices he wanted and has achieved his partnership dream! What makes his accomplishments even more amazing is that he won many of the deals during the COVID-19 lockdown in New York City where many of these new clients were located. While many salespeople during this time were afraid to sell, he was at full throttle pursuing new clients.

To this day, each time he wins a deal at the prices he wants, Rob sends me a text that simply says, "I got ink." Each time, it makes my day as I can feel him moving closer and closer to becoming a partner in the firm. I could not be more excited for him.

Here's another neat part of Rob's story. As he began achieving success, he approached the firm about splitting the cost of the coaching engagement. They agreed. The firm was so impressed by his performance that they offered to reimburse him for the entire program since it paid for itself *over fifteenfold* in a short time period. This is one of my favorite client success stories. Rob deserves all the credit for his successes. He put in the work. He made it happen!

No More Role-Playing

For professional athletes, time spent on improvement is referred to as practice. In sales, it's commonly called "role-playing." I'm not a supporter of role-playing. Salespeople dread it and they don't take it seriously. As soon as a sales manager utters those words, salespeople head for the hills. Most would rather have a root canal than participate in role-play sessions.

Yet, salespeople need to increase their knowledge and improve their skill mastery. They need to develop strong sales muscle memory. While I don't believe in role-playing, I love the concept of "skill practice." That's truly what these sessions are about. The expression "role-playing" does not communicate the exercise's importance. When professional athletes practice, they place themselves in competition-type situations. This allows them to develop muscle memory to perform flawlessly when in competition. No professional athlete on the planet shows up for a competition without having invested countless hours preparing for it. Unfortunately, many salespeople do just that. They show up without having practiced. The sales calls they conduct today are no better than they were years ago.

It's not just about practicing. To quote Vince Lombardi Jr., "Practice does not make perfect. Perfect practice makes perfect." I've seen a number of occasions when salespeople didn't perform well during skill practice sessions and then tried to excuse away their poor performance. "It's hard doing this in front of your peers," they say. But that's not hard. Hard is standing in front of Decision Influencers and not being game ready. If you can't perform in a skill practice, you are not game ready. Don't make excuses! Get better!

A professional baseball player can't stand in the batter's box waiting for a pitch while thinking about how to set their feet, the height of their hands, the positioning of their head, and the path of their swing. In a fraction of a second, all of these need to work systematically to hit the ball out of the park.

The same holds true for a salesperson. If, during a sales call, you are thinking about what questions to ask and what to say, you aren't closely listening to your DI. These meetings are not the time to think about questions and messaging. If your attention isn't 100 percent focused on the conversation with the DI, you are guaranteed to strike out. Where is that sales call mastery to be developed? It is accomplished during skill practice sessions.

Imagine you are going on a sales call to meet with a senior executive. During the call, you fumble over your elevator pitch, make an error when positioning your differentiators, and fault when responding to their concerns. If salespeople invest in themselves, the likelihood of these mistakes happening is nil. They don't even have to think about how to handle the sales call. "Sales muscle memory" takes over, allowing them to concentrate exclusively on their DI.

> Curse the practice sessions all you want, but come payday you'll be glad you did it.

I'm not suggesting that anyone loves skill practice sessions any more than kids love broccoli. Many professional athletes despise practice sessions. But just like mom made you eat your vegetables because they made you stronger, you need to participate in these sessions on a regular basis to become a stronger salesperson. Curse the practice sessions all you want, but come payday, you'll be glad you did it!

Insatiable Learning

It may take professional athletes several months or even years to make the slightest improvement. That's another difference between them and salespeople. Salespeople have the opportunity to improve almost instantly. The fact that you are reading this book says you are part of the small percentage of salespeople who recognize the importance of upping their game. You should be commended for that. However, here's my question for you, given this is the last chapter of the book.

What are you going to do with what you have read?

While I do hope you enjoyed reading *Sell Different!*, "enjoyment" was not my primary goal in writing this book. My hope is that you take the tools I've provided and do something meaningful with them to elevate your selling game. My recommendation is that you go back through the book, highlighting sections and dog-earing pages that you feel are appropriate for you. Trying to implement all these concepts and strategies at one time is unrealistic and will cause you unnecessary frustration.

To take advantage of the *Sell Different!* strategies, work on one chapter at a time, add it to your sales game, and practice it. As the old saying goes, "Amateurs practice until they get it right. Professionals practice until they can't get it wrong." With that approach, you will experience significant improvement in performance as you implement each of these strategies. Make each one of the *"Sell Different!"* strategies your own.

Don't stop your learning journey with this book. Keep reading sales books and blogs. Watch sales videos. Study your competitors. Develop mastery of your DIs. Become a student of the game of sales. Challenge yourself to be a better salesperson tomorrow than you were today. Most important, *Sell Different!*

SKILL DEVELOPMENT *SELL DIFFERENT!* CONCEPT

Invest the time to make yourself a better salesperson today than you were yesterday.

SELL DIFFERENT! CONCEPTS

1.   BUYING EXPERIENCE *SELL DIFFERENT!* CONCEPT

Be genuine and make every Decision Influencer feel special, as if they are your only one throughout the buying experience.

2.   PROSPECTING *SELL DIFFERENT!* CONCEPT

Successful prospecting strategy requires a thoughtful approach to both the qualitative and quantitative components.

3.   BUSINESS DEVELOPMENT *SELL DIFFERENT!* CONCEPT

The "If You Were Me" strategy helps you find more of your best clients by leveraging Decision Influencer relationships that you already have.

4. REFERRALS *SELL DIFFERENT!* CONCEPT

Passive referrals are provided based on product performance, but to generate active referrals, you need a thoughtful program and salespeople properly asking for them.

5. VIRTUAL SELLING *SELL DIFFERENT!* CONCEPT

New client acquisition process accommodations and technology mastery are the keys to virtual selling success.

6. MENTOR *SELL DIFFERENT!* CONCEPT

To win more deals at the prices you want, a well-coached Mentor who is firmly committed to your solution and is heavily influential in decision-making is essential.

7. DISCOVERY *SELL DIFFERENT!* CONCEPT

Comprehensive discovery is the critical foundation needed to keep deals energized and win them at the prices you want.

8. PRICING *SELL DIFFERENT!* CONCEPT

Pursue only those accounts and Decision Influencers who will perceive meaningful value in what you sell and can create budgets rather than be constrained by them.

9. CLIENT ONBOARDING *SELL DIFFERENT!* CONCEPT

Client onboarding is the documented bridge program, connecting Decision Influencers' circumstances to your solution, neutralizing their *fear of change.*

10. PILOT PROGRAM *SELL DIFFERENT!* CONCEPT

Well-structured pilot programs help resolve Decision Influencers' trust issues and give them confidence in your company's ability to perform.

11. RECAP EMAIL *SELL DIFFERENT!* CONCEPT

Recap Emails demonstrate genuine interest in an account, help you stand out from the competition, and keep your deal on track.

12. CONQUER ACCOUNTS *SELL DIFFERENT!* CONCEPT

By focusing on selling the full range of capabilities your company offers, vulnerabilities are removed and revenue increases in your client portfolio.

13. ACCOUNT MANAGEMENT *SELL DIFFERENT!* CONCEPT

Account management is the proactive, prescriptive value offered to your clients, above and beyond the benefits of what you sell, to create client delight resulting in increased tenure, revenue, and profit.

14. PRIORITY MANAGEMENT *SELL DIFFERENT!* CONCEPT

Every minute of every day needs to be wisely invested to maximize selling time, performance, and income.

15. SKILL DEVELOPMENT *SELL DIFFERENT!* CONCEPT

Invest the time to make yourself a better salesperson today than you were yesterday.

INDEX

account management, 141–51
  analyzing client portfolios in,
    144–45
  client ranking system for, 145–48
  core purpose of, 142, 149
  customer service vs., 141–43
  determining appropriate levels of,
    149–50
  Five-Point Client Value Analysis
    in, 144–49
  to increase client retention and
    growth, 143
  prescriptive value of, 142
  tiers of services in, 148
account monitoring, 150
account profitability, in Five-Point
  Client Value Analysis, 144–46, 148
active referral leads, 38, 39
  incentives for, 42–44
  from industry salespeople, 44–45
advertising
  placement and performance of
    ads, 35–36
  for referrals, 42
advisory boards, 150
agenda, for virtual meetings, 52–53
Amazon, 136, 137
athletes, skill development in, 163–65
athletic recruiting, 2, 11
  by Augsburg University, 7–10

by Concordia St. Paul University,
    5–7
  by Hamline University, 3–4
audience, knowing your, xxiii
Augsburg University, 7–10
authenticity, 7–10
automotive industry, 7

back-office setup, for client
  onboarding, 107
Bateman, Keith, 7–10
body language, in virtual selling,
  49–51
B2B sales
  business drivers in, 83
  number of decision makers in,
    124–25
"The Business Developer's Mantra,"
  37–38
business development, 27–34
  clarity about clients you want in,
    27–29
  expectations for, 27
  "If You Were Me" strategy in,
    30–34
  mantra for, 37–38
  processing recommendations for,
    33–34
business drivers, in B2B sales, 83
buyers. *see* Decision Influencers (DIs)

revenue generation, task management
for, 156–58
Reverse Timeline approach, 111–13
risk minimization, pilot programs
for, 116
ROI (Return on Investment), 89–91
role-playing, 167

the Saboteur, 67, 69
Sales Crime Theory, 20
Sales Differentiation (Salz), xxiv
  Deal Obstacles in, 87
  Sales Crime Theory in, 20
  Target Client Profile in, 28–29
Sales Success Recipe, 84
sales task optimization, 158–60
self-honesty, in ranking mentors,
  62–63
Sell Different!
  concepts in, 171–74, *see also*
    individual concepts
  goal of, xxi
selling strategy, xxii–xxiii
  coaching mentors on, 67–70
  differentiation in, xxiv, 2–3, *see also*
    specific topics
  and key decision factors, xxiii–xxiv
"Sideview Mirror Syndrome," 112
16-day prospecting campaign,
  20–24
skill development, 163–70
  in athletes compared to
    salespeople, 163–65
  insatiable learning for, 169
  and role-playing, 167
  for sales professionals, 165–67
  skill practice for, 167–68
smiling, 57
social media, in virtual selling, 49
software industry, 7

solutions, providing, 132–33. *see also*
  conquer accounts
staffing industry, 2–3
strategic account, in Five-Point Client
  Value Analysis, 145, 147, 148
strategic solutions, providing, 132–33.
  see also conquer accounts
success
  client's definition of, 109, 119
  quantifying, 154

Target Client Profile, 28–29, 31, 89
task management, 156–60
TCO (Total Cost of Ownership),
  89–91
technology
  for pilot programs, 120
  for virtual selling, 50–53
technology training industry, 35–37
texts, business development strategy
  and, 30
time investment/management,
  153–54
timeline, for client onboarding, 108,
  111–13
timing
  in asking for referrals, 39–40
  of prospecting calls, 21
  of Recap Email, 125
  of 16-day prospecting campaign
    contacts, 22–24
Total Cost of Ownership (TCO),
  89–91
training, in client onboarding, 108
transition, in client onboarding,
  108–9
trial program. *see* pilot program
trust
  and authenticity mindset, 7, 9
  and client onboarding, 111

ABOUT THE AUTHOR

When salespeople aren't winning deals at desired levels or price points, executives and business owners turn to **Lee B. Salz**, a world-renowned sales management strategist and CEO of Sales Architects®. A recognized specialist in Sales Differentiation, Lee helps organizations win more deals at the prices they want. Working across all industries and sales types, he creates winning sales strategies for companies around the globe.

A featured columnist in The Business Journals and a media source on sales and sales management, Lee has been quoted and featured by the *Wall Street Journal*, CNN, the *New York Times*, MSNBC, ABC News, and numerous other outlets.

Lee is a frequently sought keynote speaker at association conferences, sales meetings, and virtual events. He conducts customized workshops on a wide array of sales performance topics including Sales Differentiation, salesforce development, hiring, onboarding, and compensation.

He is the bestselling, award-winning author of six books, including *Sales Differentiation* and *Hire Right, Higher Profits*.

A graduate of Binghamton University, originally from New York City and New Jersey, Lee now resides with his family in Minneapolis. When he isn't helping his clients win more deals at the prices they want, you will find him throwing batting practice to his sons, training for his next powerlifting meet, and goofing around with his dogs.

Lee can be reached at lsalz@salesarchitects.com for consulting, workshops, and keynote talks, which are available in both in-person and virtual formats. You can also follow him on the major social media platforms.